SESSIONS WITH PHILIPPIANS

Smyth & Helwys Publishing, Inc.
6316 Peake Road
Macon, Georgia 31210-3960
1-800-747-3016
© 2011 by Smyth & Helwys Publishing
All rights reserved.
Printed in the United States of America.

The paper used in this publication meets the minimum
requirements of American National Standard for Information
Sciences—Permanence of Paper for Printed Library Materials.

Library of Congress Cataloging-in-Publication Data

Prosser, Bo.
Sessions with Philippians / by Bo Prosser.
p. cm.
Includes bibliographical references and index.
ISBN 978-1-57312-579-6 (pbk. : alk. paper)
1. Bible. N.T. Philippians—Commentaries.
I. Title.
BS2705.53.P76 2011
227'.607—dc22

2011004716

Sessions *with*
●●●Philippians

Finding *Joy* in *Community*

Bo Prosser

SMYTH&HELWYS
PUBLISHING, INCORPORATED MACON, GEORGIA

Also by Bo Prosser

Lessons from the Cloth: 501 One-Minute Motivators for Leaders

Building Blocks for Sunday School Growth

Marriage Ministry: A Guidebook

Help! I Teach Youth Sunday School

Approaching a Missional Mindset

Dedication

To Nannie Prosser
who first blessed me with the joy of Rainbow and Watermelon Days.

To Mancil Ezell, Bob Fulbright, and Jack Naish
who have blessed me with the joy of intentional Congregational Ministry.

To Gail, Jamie, Katie, Sean and the "grand dogs"
who have blessed me with the joy of unconditional love.

Acknowledgments

I am grateful to the many in my "village" who have helped raise me up. Jill Jenkins first introduced me to Michael McCullar almost twenty years ago. This would be an introduction that would form a meaningful collaboration of work and teaching and now writing.

I'm extremely grateful to Michael for trusting me with one of his "babies" in this Sessions series. All of our teaching, dreaming, and late night talks have contributed to the joy of writing for this series. Michael is a trusting guide who has given me great freedom of expression in this work.

I am also grateful to the staff of Smyth & Helwys for a long and fun journey in publishing. They have guided me from project to project with great grace and enthusiasm. They have always been quick to encourage and slow to critique. They have made me a better writer, especially in the partnership of Leslie Andres. What a joy to write and have such a thoughtful editor! Thank you, Leslie, for your patience and energy. You have pushed me to clarify and re-think. I'm grateful. Thanks for an extra exclamation point or two!!

I'm grateful to Daniel Vestal and the staff of the Cooperative Baptist Fellowship. You all have encouraged me to keep at "it" and to do "it" well. I'm especially grateful for my staff in the congregational formation initiative. Your knowledge of congregational ministry inspires me and has contributed to this work. Your passion for the local church is certainly a joy to share. Thanks especially to Toni Draper for doing some of the early manuscript help.

Finally, I am grateful to God for this calling of ministry through writing. I remember my first article, about how to use a poster. What a humbling experience, and what an exciting opportunity! Thanks to all my co-writers, partners in ministry, and friends and family. You certainly are a community of joy. I am grateful!

Table of Contents

Introduction
What a Fellowship! What a Joy Divine!

There is *nothing* like a personal letter. Especially in this day of two-line emails and ten-second voice messages, a personal letter is a great gift. Each personal letter I receive goes into a file folder. Occasionally, I take them out and read them again to remind me of the special friends who care enough to send personal greetings.

The letter to the Philippians is this kind of gift. It is a personal letter written to a cherished congregation from another place and time. This letter is written from one who has fond memories of significant ministry among an endeared group of people. Yet, the letter also is filled with references about an impending reunion. There is no doubt about the special relationship between Paul and the Philippian congregation. As we get a glimpse of their relationship, perhaps we may hear Paul entering into a similar relationship with us.

This is a letter the Philippian congregation would take out and read and reread. This is a letter we can also take out from time to time and read and reread. It might be helpful to read it aloud annually to remind us of Paul's special relationship to Jesus and hear him call us into a renewed relationship too.

The letter is short by Paul's standards. He does not elaborate on themes other than his joy in Christ and in his friendship with the Philippian church. He rarely uses personal names as points of reference, speaking to the whole congregation instead. Paul makes clear the centrality of his faith in Christ Jesus, his love for the Philippian church, and his joy in serving both Christ and their church.

The Setting

Philippi was a Roman city founded by Philip, the father of Alexander the Great, and was strategically located as a gateway from Europe to Asia. The city was rich with the culture of Rome and the money of the empire. There were gold and silver mines in the area, which led to buying, selling, and banking. The money of trade, the strategic placement of the military, and the pride of Roman citizenship made Philippi a grand city. The Philippian Christians had to deal with their place in this culture. There was joy in being a citizen of Philippi, which may have been one of the reasons Paul's joy in them was so prevalent.

Paul first came to Philippi on his second missionary journey (see Acts 16). He found himself in the midst of a rich and diverse culture. The group of believers there struggled with their identity as part of the grandeur of the Roman culture.

To this church, Paul wrote in Philippians 3:20, "But our citizenship is in heaven." In the greatness of the city, the congregation was challenged to stay focused on the priorities of their faith. They indeed remained faithful to Paul, sharing consistently in their offerings of money and prayers.

However, because of their relationship with Paul, they also endured persecution. To the Romans, this ragtag band of cultic believers was an irritation. To the leaders within Judaism, they were heretics, turning their backs on the religion of their family and their lifestyle. To their families, they were deserters, abandoning not only their faith but also their heritage.

They faced daily stress from Romans, Jews, friends, and family. They were mocked, persecuted, misunderstood, and forsaken. They faced daily arguments with friends and family who could not understand their new faith. They faced daily ridicule from those who held allegiance to other powers. They suffered from those who loved them and feared them and misunderstood them. Some of those all at the same time!

Paul wrote to these believers urging them not to fear, but to endure and hold firm in their faith and in their unity (1:27-28). In Philippians 3:1, he urges them to stay strong in their faith and not to give in to the seduction of Judaism.

The Letter of Joy

Philippians is a pastoral epistle. Paul likely wrote it while under house arrest in Rome between the mid-fifties to mid-sixties AD. With a heart of gratitude and affection for this congregation, he wrote because he was concerned for the people's welfare. Additionally, he mentioned the return of Epaphroditus (a member of the Philippian congregation who had delivered provisions to Paul) to them, asking them to honor him for his service to Paul. Finally, as Paul faced death in Rome, he wanted to ensure that the congregation would stand firmly in Christ, unified by the truth of the gospel.

Facing imprisonment and impending death, Paul still wrote with joy, in joy, and about joy. He was thankful for the friendship and support of the Philippian congregation. He was grateful for the servanthood of Timothy and Epaphroditus. He was filled with the joy of Christ. He wrote to encourage this congregation in the same joy.

This is a personal epistle. Paul wrote with the heart of a pastor. Yet it is not a private letter. Paul knew this letter would be read by the church leaders. He also knew this letter would be read aloud in the congregation. In fact, this would probably be read aloud in several congregational settings. It would be treasured as a personal gift from their beloved missionary.

His letter is filled with many elements of public worship such as hymns, prayers, and doxologies. The final verses of the letter (Phil 4:10-20) are some of the most moving in all of Scripture. Paul writes to inform. He writes to encourage. He writes to lift up the name of Jesus and call the hearer to the joy of community.

He clearly wrote the letter to be read aloud, either as a whole or in segments, as part of the worship experience. Paul wrote for the reader but also for the hearer. He knew that portions of the letter would be used to exhort the members of the church while in worship. He hoped his words would echo throughout the church for years and serve as a guide and a comfort to this special congregation.

He did not write this for you and me. We are the recipients of a blessing that only has come to us in the providence of God. While Paul did not write this for us specifically, we are blessed today by his words.

This is a particular epistle. Paul was not writing to the "church universal" or to the "church of the future." He wrote to a specific congregation at a particular place and time. He addressed his words with no thought of them ending up in a "Holy Bible."

He deeply cared about this congregation with whom he shared a special bond. He was filled with joy for them and concerned for them. They had supported his ministry at every step of his journey. Paul wrote to thank them for what they meant to him, to share some of himself with them, and to give comfort and joy to a church that had "been partners in giving, receiving, working, and rejoicing. Even now, the same agony Paul knows is that which they also are experiencing. This fact more than any other accounts for what some call the beauty, others the simplicity, others the warmth, and yet others the spirituality of the letter" (Craddock, 7).

The Outline

The main purpose of this letter is to share joy. From the greeting until the benediction, Philippians is a letter of joy and gratitude to a congregation for their partnership and their prayers. Paul was joyful for the ongoing support from this congregation, for the friendships he shared with many of them, and for the goodness of God in all their lives.

However, Paul was also concerned. He realized the problems that could arise in a congregation. He understood that self-sufficiency could quickly become self-centeredness. He held up Christ as the example for the congregation, emphasizing self-denial and self-sacrifice. As we examine our lives, perhaps we will see that we too need to embrace these characteristics.

The following themes will guide our journey through these sessions with Philippians. May we hear the voice of Paul speaking to us even as we hear him exhorting his beloved Philippian congregation.

Joyful Greetings, 1:1-2
Joyful Prayer, 1:3-11
Joyful Victory, 1:12-26
Joyful Unity, 1:27–2:13
Joyful Models, 2:14-30
Joyful Living, 3:1–4:9
Joyful Gratitude, 4:10-20
Joyful Benediction, 4:21-23

Life Lessons

1. Where is home for you? Where did you grow up? What church formed you? What do you remember best about home?

_____

_____

_____

_____

_____

_____

_____

2. What gives you joy? What does joy look like, sound like, feel like, taste like? What color is joy? What shape? (Obviously, there are no right or wrong answers here.)

_____

_____

_____

_____

_____

_____

_____

3. If you were going to write a letter to a church, how would you encourage its people? What words or word pictures would you use? Consider writing a letter of encouragement and affirmation to your church.

_____

_____

_____

_____

_____

_____

_____

4. How can we support the work of a missionary? Make a list of ways to help. As you go through this study, determine how many of these tasks the Philippians shared with Paul. How can you share with a missionary today?

_____

_____

_____

_____

_____

_____

_____

5. What do you hope to learn in this study of sessions with Philippians? Write a prayer of your hopes for learning and personal growth as you begin. Pray that God will open your heart to the truths of joyful living.

_____

_____

_____

_____

_____

_____

Joyful Greetings

Social networking is all the rage. Facebook continues to grow at an amazing pace, reaching most of the civilized world. Twitter engages community with instant interactions. Flickr invites us to share pictures from our daily activities. With a computer, a laptop, a smart phone, or an e-reader, one can communicate immediately with friends all around the world. Last week I sat in Atlanta and conversed with friends in Cuba, Chile, Texas, California, and Canada.

Yet virtual communications are typically short. Twitter mandates that a post be no more than 140 characters. Facebook lets you post only a few ideas at a time. When I respond to an e-mail, I try to do so in three sentences or less. Most text messages are three to four words, and they are often abbreviated or shorthand.

We live in a society that is less formal and more impersonal than at any other time. We live in a world where we often have more "virtual" relationships than real ones. Several people I know have thousands of Facebook friends yet are afraid to walk out their front door. We tend to relate better and more consistently to the people we don't know than to our own families or friends who sit next to us on the church pew. That was not the case in Paul's day.

The letter to the Philippians opens in the manner consistent with letters of Paul's time. Paul is writing to the Philippians with whom he became acquainted around AD 52. They are a beloved congregation, and he wants to encourage them even as they have encouraged and supported him. He is probably writing about ten years after his first visit. While scholars are not certain as to the time or place of this writing, the best insights seem to point to somewhere between AD 60 and AD 62. As in all of his thirteen biblical letters, he begins with his autograph. In v. 1, Paul identifies himself directly and mentions his assistant and friend, Timothy. He authenticates the letter with labels the Philippians would have recognized. He gives them his personal name and the name of Timothy. He also uses the definitive Christian references "servants of Jesus Christ" and "saints in Christ Jesus." Timothy has been his assistant in the beginning work at Philippi. Paul would have used the term "servant" frequently in his work with them. The Philippians would see Paul's handiwork and testimony in the opening lines of his letter. This is not an anonymous letter sent under Paul's name. This is not a "copycat" epistle sent out broadly to churches in the area. This is a personal letter from a friend to his friends. He writes to the bishops and deacons and the "saints" of the congregation at Philippi. He knows to whom he writes, and they know who writes to them. He is personal in his salutations.

Even with the common elements, this letter is different from others Paul penned. In the letter to the Roman congregation, he uses six verses to list all his credentials. In other letters, Paul writes with varying elements of impersonality and directness. In this letter, however, Paul omits his credentials and gives personal direction to the church leaders. In Romans and Corinthians, Paul mostly writes to audiences with whom he would not have been familiar. But the Philippian congregation is known and beloved.

Paul shares a "Twitter-like" greeting with them. There is no need for a grand elaboration of his credentials. He has no need to certify his authorship. He and the Philippians are linked heart to heart; they know each other with a certain degree of intimacy.

Paul is clearly close to this congregation. He knows them and is known by them. There is an indication in the words, both in manner and brevity, that lets us know this is a special group of believers linked in the love of Christ to one of their beloved ministers.

"Friends"

In this letter, Paul is simply "Paul." The congregation knows him; he knows them. He doesn't have to introduce Timothy; the congregation also knows him and has worked with him. He writes to the leadership of the congregation. He knows them too. They are the decision-makers who have supported him and have led the church to continue supporting him. Paul's greeting indicates a long-standing friendship between a missionary and a supporting church. He has been in their homes and in their hearts. They are the sustainers of his joy, even as he endures prison and faces death.

Yet Paul will not let his friendship and joy for these people get in the way of proclaiming the joy of the gospel. He gives his autograph as "Paul, servant of Jesus Christ . . . ." Paul will not let the congregation escape the tug of the gospel on all of them. Part of his continuing joy is the friendship they share in Christ Jesus and the ministry of being a servant of Christ.

At later points in the letter, Paul encourages the church to imitate him. He is referring back to this servanthood. Paul is never far from his salvation experience and call to ministry. He doesn't want the Philippian congregation to wander far from their call to service, either, so he continually challenges them to stay strong in the joy of Jesus.

In a thoughtful act, Paul also includes Timothy in the autograph. The leader of the team includes his partner. This too is evidence of Paul's servanthood to Jesus. Timothy is not assumed to be a co-author of the letter, but he is considered a partner in the ministry. Timothy is also a source of joy to Paul and eventually becomes one of Paul's most trusted colleagues. As a servant of Christ, Paul sets aside his own ego to treat Timothy as an equal, a partner in ministry.

Friendship is an important aspect of our lives. We need friends! We need people we can call at three o'clock in the morning and ask for help. We need friends who will weep when we weep and celebrate when we celebrate. Paul knows Timothy and the members of the Philippian church are these kinds of friends. His affirmation and love for them is evident throughout the letter.

"Saints"

Paul affirms his friends in the Philippian congregation as "saints" (v. 1). What an affirmation to a congregation that struggled to remain faithful as citizens of the Roman Empire! Because of their close relationship with Paul, the persecution directed at him is also directed at the church. By calling them "saints," Paul admonishes them to continue on in their ministry and their witness.

This salutation is not given lightly. "Saints" is typically a term reserved for "holy ones" who have been claimed by God. In some instances, this is simply a reference to the moral character of the person. In this particular instance, Paul is not using sentimental language. He is definitely (and intimately) connected to the Philippians and knows that the people are saintly. God has claimed them, they have claimed God, and they are living as godly people—

upright and morally driven. They are faithful in their love and their witness even as they live in less than divine conditions.

With this distinction, Paul challenges the congregation to continue to be different from the other citizens of the city. Christians are different because of their allegiance to God in Jesus Christ. Living as saints helps these Philippian Christians focus on the teachings of Jesus. As saints, they are always acting in the love of Jesus, living out his ways. Their "saintliness" is a result of being called out by God and of responding in faith.

This divine call is issued to all of us. Our response to follow and to live with intentionality "in Christ" must also be present. The call to live as "saints" is in direct opposition to the prominent way of life today. Too many of us are running in ten different directions and being distracted by too many "priorities." We have forgotten our calling and the joy of our salvation. Too often we forsake our calling to be "saints." We tend to let ourselves off the hook by striving just to be good people.

But Christianity must continue to be more than an admonition to "do good." Paul and the Philippians lived every day to the fullest for the glory of God. Their lifestyle was threatened by persecution, public ridicule, and even death. Paul faces death even as he writes to this congregation.

We may not fully understand the depth of such a commitment. We all understand the divine call at some level, but few of us commit to such a call. Most of us have yet to comprehend the depths of our response in order to be considered a "saint"! Simply being a good person is not being a saint. Being a minister or church leader is not being a saint.

Living as a saint means making sacrifices and immersing oneself into the ministry of Jesus. Living as a saint means separating oneself from the world and "selling out" to the work of God. The Philippians believed in an extraordinary faith. They were able to thrive in the face of difficult situations. For Paul and his followers, being a saint happened in the course of living one's life; it was not a title bestowed upon a person at death! The affirmation that there were "saints" in the Philippian church means the church *lived* faithfully. The people did not surrender to the external conditions, and they were certainly not dying as a fellowship.

The Philippian church was a missional congregation—one that participated in the mission of God. They were attuned to God's call and the work of God, and they were finding ways to involve themselves in this work. A church is on a missional journey "not because it votes at a church conference to do something nice for others but because mission is at the heart of the God it worships" (Bugg, 3). The missional journey reminds us that we are on mission with God and with one another, intentionally moving forward. This is the divine call to sainthood, and it is a picture of the Philippian congregation.

"In Christ Jesus"

Paul now shifts from the picture of "sainthood" to that of being "in Christ Jesus." This familiar Pauline characterization is found repeatedly in his letters and reflects the depth of human response to the divine call. The phrase "in Christ Jesus" occurs more than forty times in the letter. The phrase "in Christ" occurs more than thirty times. And, the phrase "in the Lord" is used more than fifty times. Paul stresses that they were God's people through Jesus the Christ. He will not let them forget that they are the people of Jesus, living their lives in Jesus. For Paul, these people are in a deep and meaningful relationship with Jesus. He emphasizes their "saintliness" almost 150 times in these four short chapters. Do you hear Paul's joy in this congregation? Do you hear the affirmation he constantly pours out on them?

To be "in Christ Jesus" is both a personal commitment and a corporate union. The one who claims Christ as Lord and Savior is individually linked to the Son of God and commits to live in and by the rule of the Lord. This individual expression of response then binds one with the people of God. To be "in Christ Jesus" indicates both a personal relationship and the gift of community.

In sin, we find ourselves alienated from God and from the Christian community. In Christ Jesus, we find ourselves embraced by God and the Christian community. We are never alone or alienated when we profess faith in Christ Jesus. This Philippian congregation is a small group of believers. They are persecuted by Rome and Jewish leaders. They are outcasts from their own families. All around them they are isolated and tested, yet they are reminded by the missionary who founded them and loves that they are a community of joy because of their lives in Christ. The Philippian congregation is a community of imperfect people who are renewed in the power of Christ. Maybe the same could be said of us!

In sin, we drift in the chaos of the world and find ourselves tossed to and fro by any wind that blows. "In Christ Jesus," we have direction and clarity about who we are and what we are to do. As congregational Christians and as individual Christians, we are to be engaged in the mission of God. We hear both the "Great Commission" of Matthew 28 and the "Great Commandment" of Matthew 22, and we strive to live these out in the context of our daily lives.

"Bishops and Deacons"

Paul chooses to address directly the "bishops and deacons" in Philippi. This is the only place in his letters to churches where he singles out the leadership. The Greek actually translates "overseers and assistants." Let us understand that he is talking to those who have been set apart for leadership—the decision-makers. Again, due to the small size of the congregation, he is probably addressing no more than three to five people.

We would do well not to impose our cultural sensitivity to these words on the Philippian church. It is easy to make the mistake of reading the Bible through our perspectives and impose our experiences on Scripture. The offices of "bishop and deacon" would not come into formal congregational structure until at least a generation or two after the writing of this letter. Paul simply addresses the leadership of the Philippian church.

However, the purpose of a direct address to these leaders is puzzling. Perhaps Paul writes to acknowledge a formal receipt of the offering the church had given him. Perhaps he writes to give special encouragement to those who had particular leadership responsibilities. Both bishops and deacons would have labored in the midst of the challenges within and outside the congregation. Paul speaks to those who lead the work of the congregation. He does not address "status" but those who serve. This is consistent with Paul's designation for himself in verse 1: "Paul and Timothy, servants of Christ Jesus."

Most likely, Paul writes to give encouragement to the leadership of the church at Philippi. As we will see later, for all its good qualities, the church was experiencing discord. While we aren't certain what it was, we know the division would have strained the congregational leaders. Paul singles out the leadership in order to assure them of his support. It is also a way to alert them to his counsel, and it would have served as a notice to those causing the tension to correct their behavior.

Since the congregation would hear this announcement in the letter over and over again in worship, Paul's direct mention of the leadership puts everyone on notice. The approach to leadership is service. The approach to congregational community is servanthood. The status of all within the congregation is "in Christ Jesus." Paul's salutation to them expresses that, while separated by distance, they are still united in the bond of Jesus. Whatever disagreements and tensions exist in the fellowship must be corrected.

"Grace and Peace"

The phrase "grace and peace" (v. 2) is the standard signature of Paul's writings. His double greeting represents the best of his life and is somewhat a testimony to his personal heritage. The greeting also represents the best of anyone's life in Christ. Paul is reminding this beloved congregation that the whole Christian experience is made possible only from God through faith in Jesus Christ.

"Grace" is representative of his deep Hellenistic roots. Paul is a Roman citizen brought up in the ways of the empire. Yet this grace is also representative of his Christian life. The miracle of grace had certainly happened to him personally.

Paul was once a violent persecutor of Christians. Without the grace of God in Christ, Paul would still live in the shameful torment of his past. While God's grace had a powerful individual effect on Paul, grace is never understood in isolation. It has to be a blessing between persons in relationship. In offering this blessing of "grace" to the Philippian believers, Paul acknowledges his continued relationship with God the Father and the Lord Jesus Christ. He remembers the joy of his salvation and also calls the community to a memory of their joy.

How often you and I refuse this grace! We acknowledge God's grace as active in the world, but we negate the miracle of it in our own lives. There is no future and certainly nothing beneficial about continuing to punish ourselves with the pain of our mistakes. Paul had put good people to death purely for religious fanaticism, and yet not only did he accept God's grace but he also forgave himself. This was not done lightly.

What we know about Paul assures us that internalizing this grace is important to him and the Philippians. He consistently shares grace as part of the salutation. He desires that the Philippians accept the grace of Christ in the same way that Paul has learned to accept this grace. Paul internalized this grace after agonizing over his own sinfulness. He encourages the Philippians to do the same. Basically, Paul is encouraging these beloved friends that they are indeed friends to him, servants of Jesus, and children of God. You and I might hear Paul's words, too, and accept this gift of grace as well.

"Peace" signifies Paul's deep Jewish roots. The great *shalom* (peace) of God is the result of the great grace of God. Peace here does not mean the absence of war or trouble. It does not mean the escape from toil and struggle; after all, Paul writes this letter from prison.

Rather, this peace is the recognition of reconciliation with God, self, and others by the grace that comes through Jesus the Christ. Peace for Paul means being at home with God. Additionally, like grace, this peace is never recognized in isolation. It is a blessing that emerges from a relationship with God. Paul is grateful for God's forgiveness, for the peace this forgiveness brings, and for the love of God through Christ. This love continually burns within Paul for his beloved Philippian congregation and, indeed, for the whole world. (See 1 Corinthians 13 for Paul's spectacular treatise on love.)

Conclusion

In two short verses, Paul conveys deep feelings of love for this congregation, encouragement to its leaders, and a testimony of grace and peace. Paul gives joyful greetings to a congregation that has supported him materially and spiritually. He shares "holy hugs" with friends he appreciates and for whom he is concerned. He knows them by name, by their ministry, and by their faith. What a blessing to have someone care so deeply!

Paul has been moved by the power of the love of God in Christ for the Philippian congregation. This power of love stirs within each of us as we come to a redemptive relationship with God. It moves us to reach out to others, inviting them into such a relationship. Paul remembers, as should each of us, that this is something we cannot achieve by ourselves. We cannot attain this power of love in isolation. It can only happen in community!

Holding on to faith in community is not an easy prospect. At times, it seems much easier to withdraw from community and be silent. Too often, while others certainly share a blessing, they also share pain and hurt. But that is life, is it not? Few of us are called to the isolation of a monastery. We are called to be Samaritans who journey alongside, encounter, and even search for those in need on our pathway. Relationships can be painful, but my friends bring meaning to my life and, more often than not, they have given me grace.

As our world becomes more connected by the immediacy of the Internet and other social media, many of us have made "friends" with people all around the world. As our conversations become limited to two or three thoughts, abbreviated text "emoticons," or even 140 characters, we need to remember that meaningful conversation goes much deeper. We do well to remember the importance of real, tangible relationships. We should sit across a table from a loving friend at the coffee shop and refuse to glance at our cell phones. We should strive to share others' tears and their smiles. As we struggle with the ways of the world, we should try to live more into the grace, peace, and love of God through Jesus the Christ.

Life Lessons

1. Who knows you well enough that you only have to use your *first* name in giving a greeting? How does this signify a depth of relationship? How have these more in-depth relationships affected your life?

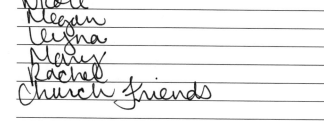

Family / Nicole,
I have love & support
and can turn to them
when in need.

2. Which friends mean the most to you? Have you told them? Perhaps part of this study might include writing personal letters to these special people.

Nicole
Megan
leigha
Mary
Rachel
Church friends

3. How much time do you spend in "social networking"? How much time do you spend in "face-to-face networking"? When is the last time you simply visited with someone? What did you notice about the person? The setting? The situation?

Not Much   June.

4. Who are the "saints" in your church? How do they live? Do you live in their example? In whose example are you living? What stands in the way of your being recognized as a saint? What needs to happen for you to move toward more saintly living?

5. What offices or positions of leadership do you hold in your church? Are these positions of power or of service? How does Paul introduce himself? What does it mean to be a "servant of Christ"? Why do you think Paul singles out the "bishops and deacons" in this letter? What might Paul be saying to us as well?

6. What does "grace" mean for your life? When have you received grace? Who gave it? What did it do for you? Who needs to receive grace from you? What keeps you from sharing it?

_____

_____

_____

_____

_____

_____

_____

7. What does "peace" mean for your life? When have you received peace? Which comes first, "grace" or "peace"? Why do you think so?

_____

_____

_____

_____

_____

_____

_____

8. For Paul, "grace and peace" is the perfect greeting for sharing his testimony of God's love and his motivation for his own love. Do you agree? Why or why not? Based on this model for sharing testimony and love, what might your two-word greeting be?

_____

_____

_____

_____

_____

_____

_____

9. To what have you been called? When did God *first* call you? How has God called you since? How has God gifted you for service? How are you responding?

_____
_____
_____
_____
_____
_____
_____
_____

We all need reminders that we are worthy. In my counseling days I used to hand out "IALAC" cards to my clients. These were business cards with my name and contact info on one side and the words "I Am Loving and Capable" on the other. I told them that whenever they began to feel unloved or devalued, they were to pull out the card and remind themselves of their worth.

As I mentioned earlier, I also save correspondence I've received through the years. These are letters, notes, and cards of affirmation and support. I place them in what I call my "honey pot" folder (with special thanks to Winnie the Pooh). On bad days, insecure days, lonely days, I go to my "honey pot" to remind me that I am loving and capable (IALAC), that the sky is not falling, and that this will soon pass. I'm grateful to my friends over the years who have blessed me with their love and affirmation through these personal cards and letters.

Philippians is a "honey pot" kind of letter from Paul. It is undoubtedly a letter the recipients read aloud again and again in worship. As the Philippians struggled at times to remember the joy of their salvation, this letter is a constant reminder of their goodness and Paul's delight in their friendship. Hearing the words of affirmation and challenge from Paul helped the congregation stay focused on their core values and their constant mission. This section of Paul's letter is evidence of his intense love and support for the Philippian believers.

His words are deeply personal and sincere. There is no doubt of his love and constant thoughts for these friends. His thanksgiving (v. 3), joy (v. 4), gratitude (v. 5), confidence (v. 6), affection (v. 7), and longing for them all (v. 8) show the depth of their relationship.

Their *koinonia,* their form of community, demonstrates the *agape* of Christ's love, which runs much deeper than fellowship between a missionary and a congregation.

What a beautiful model of friendship Paul expresses in these six verses! He tells the Philippians specifically how deeply he loves them. He could have simply said, "I love you!" but instead he goes to great lengths, spelling out his love in precise ways. We often tell others we love them, but our words somehow ring empty. Here, Paul leaves no doubt about the depth of his love for these believers.

Paul is in an ongoing relationship with this congregation. They are partners in ministry who have given monetary support to him. They are warriors in prayer, and they are encouragers of each other in life. What a blessing this was to the congregation and to Paul!

There is joy in Paul's prayer. His remembrance of this congregation is filled with joyful memories. Paul emphasizes his continual "rejoicing" in his relationship with the Philippians. They are partners in grace, in ministry, and with Christ. The joy of the Lord is their strength, and the Spirit of the Lord is their guide.

Thanksgiving

Paul is thankful for this Christian community that has supported him. He is certainly grateful for their monetary gift. He is also grateful for their partnership in the gospel and their support, tangible and spiritual, of his ministry. As a struggling missionary and a gentleman, he expresses his thanks.

Yet, even before Paul begins thanking the congregation, he thanks God. Paul praises God for God's grace and love. Thanking God comes naturally for some of us, but not so naturally for others. Some of us look to God and ask, "Is that all there is? Can't you do better?" Paul immediately recognizes that all gifts come from God and that all gifts are blessings. He thanks God! Next, he gives thanks for this church, and then he moves to intercession and petition.

Paul's prayer offers a strong model for us. Our prayers often focus on what God needs to do for us. We get lost in the many prayer requests that we lay at the feet of God. But prayer must be more than our "shopping list of needs" delivered to God to be fulfilled. Paul prays with thanksgiving, even from prison, for all the goodness in his life. He regards every life situation as an opportunity for joy and thanksgiving. Certainly, Paul has a "shopping list," yet he models thanksgiving rather than personal requests.

I think God is pleased when we come with prayers of petition. God loves to hear our requests. I also think God is pleased when we pray with thanksgiving. When we pray with thanksgiving, "we give glory to God for what God has done for us. In praise, we give glory to God for who God is" (Foster, 83).

Paul's thanksgiving goes much deeper. He is continually thankful. The Philippian congregation was a constant source of support and strength for him. They are at the "top" of his prayer list. Paul's prayer of thanksgiving is both for the gifts they have shared and for the prayers they offer. Paul knows (as does this congregation) that he has invested in them. They are important to him. He also knows that they have invested in him—that he is important to them. Again, their friendship is much deeper than a casual relationship; they share in the *koinonia* of God. The joys of "giving and receiving" are reasons for thanksgiving and constant prayer.

Paul is linked to the Philippians both through tangible expressions of support and through emotional bonds. The congregation has shared generously with him. He is also aware that they are continuing a good work in their own community. They are truly "church" in the fullest sense—giving, receiving, praying, ministering, evangelizing, and worshiping. For this and so much more, he constantly prays joyfully with thanksgiving.

Here is perhaps a "scorecard" for how we are doing in our modern churches. How well does your church give to and share with others? How well does your church receive gifts from others? How deeply does your church pray? How do you minister and evangelize or share the gospel? How does your church worship? As you begin to answer these questions, you begin to see how effective you are as a congregation.

Perhaps the deepest link between Paul and this congregation is their partnership in sharing the good news of Jesus. By their giving and praying, they have become partners. By their missional living, they continue the good work begun in them. They are doing mission work in their own community. They are sharing the saving message of Christ with the people around them.

They are living out the ministry Paul has instilled in them. That perhaps may be the greatest gift of all. Paul finds himself in prison. He is dealing with increasingly bad health and probably with depression and self-doubt. Yet he knows in his heart of hearts that his ministry is effective. The Philippian congregation (and I suspect

Joyful Prayer

15

many others) are living out his teachings. Their generosity has endeared them to Paul, and he is grateful.

Again, Paul's joy overflows in this letter. It is directed at everyone in the congregation. Paul is no player of favorites. He loves this congregation with the depths of his soul. Paul is also joyful for the unity of the congregation. Throughout this "letter of joy," Paul will make appeals for the unity of their fellowship. Paul is joyful for all that the Philippians have done and will do with him as partners of the gospel, but the depth of his joy will be realized in their unity.

Paul's outpouring of joy would certainly draw them even closer to him. His affection and affirmation would solidify their relationship. Paul's prayer now is that this joy would also bring them closer to one another.

Paul's ultimate joy, however, is in Christ. Paul lives for Christ and shares the love of Christ with all. Paul is imprisoned because of his boldness in Christ. Paul's life is focused in Christ. And his joy is no different.

Intercession

Paul not only prays with his Philippian partners but also prays *for* them. He knows that they are sharing in the same way with him, praying with him and for him.

Paul praises God for this relationship and prays for the completion of the good work begun in them. Even more, Paul is confident that God will ready them for "the day of Jesus Christ" (the day Jesus returns). His confidence is neither arrogant nor boastful. It arises from knowing them on a deep level and from his personal knowledge of the grace of God.

Paul demonstrates the Christian witness of one beggar sharing with another. He had been a man of need, motivated by anger and misguided loyalties, but his interaction with the risen Christ began a good work in him that he now feels is moving closer to completion (see Acts 9).

Paul knows that God is guiding us all and making us ready for the day of Jesus. Perhaps Paul even sees the Philippian congregation as part of his own completion. Regardless of the timetable, Paul knows God will one day bring to completion the good work begun in all of us. Paul is "Christ confident." Paul is confident of his call to salvation that came personally and directly to him from Jesus the Christ (Acts 9). Paul is confident that he is directed daily from the leadership of Jesus the Christ (Acts 22). Paul is confident that Jesus will return (1 Thess 4). Yet, in the living of his days, he is also confident in the ongoing love of the Christ (Eph 2). For this reason and many others (vv. 6-9), Paul intercedes on behalf of this beloved congregation. They are partners in ministry, in servanthood, and in prayer. He shares his hopes for them and his prayers for them.

Why is he so fervent in his prayer support? Paul knows that none of us can complete our own lives. As self-sufficient as the Philippians may be, Paul reminds them (and us) that God is the author of our lives. Paul weaves this theme throughout the letter.

We are not created to be self-sufficient. We are created for fellowship with God and "neighbor." Jesus emphasizes this in the parable of the rich man (Luke 12:19-20). Certainly Jesus calls us to pay more attention to those around us, our neighbors, than to our self-sufficiency, the riches we store up for ourselves. And, in Jesus' conversation with the lawyer (in Luke 10:25-37), Jesus again reminds us to be self-sacrificing and concerned for others more than ourselves. Paul would put an exclamation to this in his great chapter on love in 1 Corinthians 13. In today's technologically savvy world, we tend to forget that we are mere stewards of this "garden." Paul intercedes for the Philippians in order that they would remember who is in charge of their destiny. God calls us to faithfulness in the journey. Paul's prayer is that the Philippians would remember to depend upon one another, and, even more, that they would depend on God in Christ.

We would do well to remember that also. Many of us think we control our own destinies. We work hard at controlling our lives to ensure that everything happens just as we've planned. But, as is often noted, if you want to hear God laugh, tell God your plans for your life! Every time I've tried to "give God a day off," I end up on my knees asking for forgiveness in my arrogance. I need God present and evident in my life. I suspect you do too. Paul certainly did, and in the letter, he reminds the Philippians that they do as well.

Paul knows this congregation is not perfect. There are some difficulties in their fellowship, and Paul repeatedly calls them to unity. He explains that a new life and a new community come to us in Christ. The Philippians have some work to do regarding their new community. Paul's prayer of intercession is for the congregation—not for himself.

Growth in Christ

As Paul begins verse 9, he spells out his prayer, "that your love may overflow more and more." His prayer is for their growth, for their love, and for this to be a continual activity in their lives. Paul prays that they will not just love "once" but that they will love with overflowing, over and over and over. But, he is not just praying for them to love with overflowing.

Paul prays for love, knowledge, and insight. Paul prays for the Philippians to grow in the love and wisdom of Christ. As they love one another, they will grow in their love for God in Christ. As they grow in this love, they also grow in their community and in unity.

This is not empty sentiment. Love is the way we learn—not a sentimental kind of love but a deep, abiding, godly love that teaches us. Paul prays for a love that leads to a deeper understanding of life and a purer expression of ministry (see 1 Cor 13).

This growing love leads to the discernment of what is good. Paul understands the distractions of living in the midst of affluence and misdirected thoughts. He knows the traps of falling into the deception of self-sufficiency. When he intercedes on behalf of the Philippian congregation, he prays that they will fully depend on God and one another. He prays *for* them because he loves them. He prays *with* them because he loves them.

Christianity is not a journey of achievement. We are "in Christ" by the grace of God. This is not something we can achieve on our own or by manipulating God. This is contrary to the world's message, which insists that we can accomplish anything if we try hard enough. Paul would beg to differ. The truth is that we cannot save ourselves; this only happens through God in Christ. We cannot be God! Paul knows this perhaps better than anyone. We can only know the saving grace and abiding love of God in Christ. "In Christ" is key.

Being "in Christ" does not give us an advantage over those who may not be believers. We believe in a God who keeps grace alive. Being "in Christ" does not make us better than others. As we grow in Christ, we understand that we are all sinners and have fallen short of the glory of God. Being "in Christ" does not mean we have arrived as Christians. Rather, in Christ, we continue pressing on just as Paul would press on. Our task is to stay faithful in this journey, and that is a tricky task.

We often work to achieve God's affirmation. We may fall into depression when that affirmation doesn't materialize. The reward of a job well done is a chance to do more work for the Kingdom. We don't serve to gain God's love. We serve because we love God. God has made our world right not because of anything we've done. The world was made right through the sacrifice of Jesus (John 3:16). Paul knows this and encourages the Philippians to stay faithful, to press on toward the prize of a higher calling in Christ.

Prayer Partners

When I offer to friends the promise of prayer, I'm saying, "I will pray with you and for you." Praying with and for others is an honor and a blessing; it does not happen in surface relationships. Paul is closely connected to this congregation; he calls them "partners." Who is your prayer partner? Who prays for you as you pray for him or her? All of us need close friends with whom we can share from the depths of our souls.

Partnership is the bedrock of congregational life. We share partnership as stewards of the resources God has given us. We share partnership in prayer as we lift up the needs of others to our Heavenly Parent. We share partnership as we minister to the world and support the spread of the gospel. We share partnership in the love and grace of God through Christ. We cannot be faithful to the mission of God in isolation, whether as a congregation set apart or as an individual.

Notice the attitude with which Paul prays. He prays optimistically for and with the Philippians. He prays with an eye on the future. Paul is fairly certain that his time is near and that he won't see the "day of Jesus Christ." However, his desire is for himself and for the Philippians to be found blameless on that day.

For whom are you praying? With whom are you praying? With what attitude are you praying? Paul understands the benefits of prayer and urges the Philippians to stay faithful and prayerful.

Notice that not once in these verses does Paul pray for himself! Not once does he pray in the negative. Paul doesn't speak of his condition, the negative issues in the congregation, or the bad side of life. Paul begins his prayers with thanksgiving rather than petition. Paul remembers the Philippians with love and joy. We need to consider modeling our prayers after his. We need to spend more time focused on the love and joy of our friends and partners. As we pour out our prayers of joy and thanksgiving for others, we too are strengthened in praise and thanksgiving.

Life Lessons

1. We don't invest in people or causes that aren't important to us. Do you agree or disagree with this? Why? In whom or what have you invested?

_____

_____

_____

_____

_____

_____

_____

2. Examine Paul's model for expressing deep care for this congregation. He expresses continual thanksgiving (v. 3), joy (v. 4), gratitude (v. 5), confidence (v. 6), affection (v. 7), and longing for them all (v. 8). His words are more than a simple "I love you!" Who in your life needs to hear a deeper expression of love and care? How can you relate these words to them?

_____

_____

_____

_____

_____

_____

_____

3. The Philippians were church in the fullest sense—giving, receiving, praying, ministering, evangelizing, and worshiping. Are there other factors that reflect "church"? Examine this "scorecard" and consider how your church is doing.

- How well does your church give to and share with others?
- How well does your church receive gifts from others?
- How intently does your church pray?
- How do you minister and evangelize or share the gospel?
- How does your church worship?
- What can you do to lead your church to a deeper level of spirituality?

4. Are you "Christ confident"? What does this mean? How did Paul bear witness to his "Christ confidence"? How can you?

_____

_____

_____

_____

_____

_____

_____

5. What do you think enabled Paul to be able to pray more for his friends than for himself? How can we follow his lead? How was Paul able to stay faithful especially in light of his circumstances? How can we learn to have such faithfulness?

_____

_____

_____

_____

_____

_____

6. How can we learn to pray with more optimism? How can we learn to praise God for the joy our friends bring to our lives? What makes us petition God more than we praise God?

_____

_____

_____

_____

_____

_____

7. With whom in your life are you connected as closely as Paul was to the Philippians? Who are your most intimate confidants? For whom do you pray deeply?

_____

_____

_____

_____

_____

_____

_____

8. Who are your partners in the mission of God? With whom do you partner for prayer, for fellowship, and in stewardship? With whom does your congregation partner? What are the benefits of partnering?

_____

_____

_____

_____

_____

_____

_____

9. In what areas are you growing as a believer? Where do you need to grow? How will you achieve this growth? Why do you want to grow? What will be the results of your growth?

_____

_____

_____

_____

_____

_____

Joyful Victory

Today, more than half of the mail delivered is some form of direct-mail solicitation or advertising. The average household receives somewhere between twenty and twenty-five pieces each week. We get such letters in the mail every day.

They are easy to spot. Our names are misspelled or omitted and replaced by "occupant." We know the sender wants nothing more than to "ask" for something, but we open the letters anyway. I find the ones that spell my name wrong and then attempt to be friendly especially annoying. I've nearly trained myself to discard, shred, or ignore them.

Sometimes we open these letters out of curiosity, thinking we might find a good story inside. Sometimes we have to skim multiple pages to come to the point of the solicitation. Sometimes we know the letters are asking for money, but the writer never makes the point other than to fill us with guilt. Junk mail may be the most irritating form of "personal" communication in modern times.

This junk has spilled into the world of e-mail too. Electronic junk mail, known as "spam," consists of those broadly mailed notices that let us know we've won something or need to buy something or take a trip somewhere. Of course, none of the claims are true. An entire industry has grown up around collecting and selling e-mail addresses to companies who wish to send spam messages. Junk mail and spam are annoying and irritating.

This is not the case in Paul's letter to the church at Philippi. Paul dispenses quickly with "salutations," and the hearers/readers never have to wonder why he writes. The audience doesn't have to listen to ramblings before the point emerges. The Philippians' concern for him is not news; he has already received words of encouragement from them. They know he is in prison and awaiting trial. They are anxious to hear from him and to know how he is doing. Paul does not drag out introductory words. He moves quickly to engage the congregation.

He writes to thank the Philippians. He writes to encourage them to engage in the full joy of God in Christ. As mentioned earlier, his deep praise is woven throughout the letter. His gratitude to the Philippians and to God is effusive. As he begins v. 12, he gets their attention: "I want you to know, beloved . . . ."

The Progression of the Gospel

In Paul's day, and perhaps among some people today, there was a prevailing belief that the deeper one's faith, the greater one's blessings and the better one's life (see John 9:1-3; Matt 23:11-12). For Paul to find himself facing death contradicts this basic understanding of faith.

If being a person of God gets you arrested, imprisoned, and sentenced to death, where is the blessing? If serving God brings about pain, what is the point? How could God let someone like Paul suffer so harshly? If God did that to Paul, what will God do to those of us who have less faith? Yet Paul writes joyfully and confidently.

The Philippians need a word from God. Paul writes with joy to reassure his audience. God is still God of the universe and of daily life! Only God can reverse the primitive thoughts of people. Only God in the Holy Spirit can help "the church experience the miraculous shift of attitude from assuming that wherever the Lord is there is no suffering to believing that wherever there is suffering there the Lord is" (Craddock, 25). Paul may be in prison, but the gospel is not. Paul may be suffering physically, but the gospel is alive and well. The gospel is what prospers for Paul.

Note again the intimacy with which Paul writes. The Philippian congregation is indeed a "beloved" community (v. 12, NRSV). They have waited for news of the physical, emotional and spiritual condition of their friend. They are worried about him. His writing does not disappoint them! He assures the congregation that everything that has happened to him has helped spread the gospel. Everything he is going through feeds the joy of his faith.

Paul may be in prison, but his spirit is not. The missionary may be under arrest, but the message is not. Paul speaks with joy and affirmation. God is using these bad circumstances for the progression of the gospel.

Paul speaks boldly: the bad circumstances he faces are actually God's blessings on his ministry. The prison in which Paul finds himself paradoxically gives him freedom to share the gospel with less restraint. With intimacy, joy, and confidence, Paul refuses to let his circumstances get in the way of the spread of the gospel. Paul's imprisonment is in Christ, for Christ; and Paul's courage and confidence have spread to "most everyone," both in the guard and in the broader Roman culture (v. 13).

Paul's message echoes throughout the Philippian church and beyond: "We can preach the gospel anywhere, everywhere, at any time. And God will bring the blessings!" The missionary message cannot be contained.

Paul is "Christ confident"! His confidence leads to joy, optimism, and praise. It also leads to faithful service. We often let the "prisons" in which we find ourselves keep us from faithful service. We lose the joy of our salvation and think we are unworthy and useless to God's kingdom. Paul knew that regardless of his human condition, God through Christ loved him unconditionally. But his confidence is not just about unconditional love. Paul has searched his soul and faced his own sinfulness. In so doing, he accepts the unconditional love and grace of Christ. Paul is confident in the saving grace of Christ. He is confident in the guidance of Christ. He is confident in the return of Christ. In the meantime, he is confident that he is living in Christ. Paul would not be robbed of joy or freedom even in prison. Paul realizes that the source of freedom is Christ; the source of joy is Christ. Of this and so much more in faith, Paul is confident in Christ Jesus.

Paul gave witness of his faith to the guards, to fellow prisoners, and to others in the faith who needed strengthening. If Paul could witness boldly while in prison, then certainly other Christians can share their faith in difficult circumstances. When Christ is proclaimed, the blessings of God abound, and that is a joyful victory.

Preachers—Competitors and Partners

Paul assures his beloved Philippians that his imprisonment is not in vain. He is confident that the gospel is spreading. He is hopeful that his witness has given courage to other Christians in the area. Finally, he reports that even some of his rivals are proclaiming Christ with greater boldness. What exactly does this mean?

Paul's imprisonment led many other preachers of the day to renew their efforts in preaching and evangelizing. Many preached due to envy or rivalry (vv. 15, 17). Perhaps these competitors were jealous of Paul's success. Perhaps they were angry that, even as a criminal, Paul was still the headliner. Whatever their motivation, maybe they sensed a chance to get ahead and enhance their reputations.

This is not unusual. Then as much as now, when one voice is silenced, many others rush to fill the void. Paul was out of the way in prison. The competitors sensed a chance to increase their own fame and fortune, and they responded accordingly.

What is unusual is Paul's attitude toward these competitors. In his letter to the Philippians, he does not condemn them. He does not challenge their theology or the soundness of their preaching. He only questions their motives. He rejoices that they are at least (and at last) proclaiming with a boldness they have not shown previously (v. 18).

There is also a second group of preachers who are proclaiming out of good will (vv. 15-16). Possibly, Paul is referring to partners who have "stepped up their ministry" because of his absence. They may not agree with Paul on every point or support his ministry specifically, but they love the gospel and have become more fervent in Paul's absence. All that matters to Paul is that Christ Jesus is preached.

Paul has the right attitude. He realizes that his rivals seek to exploit his imprisonment for their gain. He realizes that many still question him due to his days as a persecuting Pharisee. He realizes that there are differing degrees of theological perspectives. Ultimately, though, none of this matters to him.

What matters is his sense of urgency for the gospel. Even though Paul is in prison, the gospel has prospered. Even though Paul's competitors preach with mixed motives, the gospel has prospered. Paul knows only one direction: "Keep preaching Jesus." Paul knows only one attitude: "Rejoice in whatever means are used to share the good news."

Paul recognizes the power of the gospel. Even when those with less than honorable motives or differing theologies proclaim the good news, the gospel is transformational. As "human" as the church might be, led by unholy people with less than holy attitudes, transformation happens when Christ is proclaimed. The Holy Spirit is powerful enough to overcome any barriers, and this leads to joyful victory.

Joy and Hope

Paul is filled with the hope of Christ. He is "Christ confident." His body may be imprisoned, but his mind and spirit are rejoicing in the hope of his deliverance. Paul seems to be at peace with his imprisonment. Instead of dwelling on his difficult situation, he looks forward to a greater fulfillment of his salvation.

Paul's joy and hope are found in several areas. The first is his knowledge. Paul is secure in his faith and in his life. He hopes not to embarrass the gospel in these days of trial, yet he knows in his mind and heart that he is firmly rooted in Christ (v. 20). His knowledge has led him into a deep relationship with Jesus and allowed him to give witness to those seeking a relationship with Jesus.

The second source of this joy and hope is found in the prayers of the Philippians (v. 19). Paul's letters are filled with pleas for prayers and with thanksgiving for prayers (e.g., 2 Cor 1:11; Rom 15:30-32; 1 Thess 5:25.) He calls his "prayer partners" by many names: "beloved," "brethren," and "friends." For Paul, this is an intimate bond. He is close to his churches and depends on the strength that comes not only from his own prayers but also from the prayers of his friends. There is nothing more special or energizing than the prayers of others lifting us up, holding us gently, and interceding for us in love.

The third source of joy and hope for Paul is his faith in the "Spirit of Jesus Christ" (v. 19). Paul perhaps is using the term, "the Spirit of Christ" in reference to the Holy Spirit. It is the Holy Spirit that undergirds the prayers offered by his friends. The Holy Spirit brings courage and strength, providing the boldness Paul needs to keep proclaiming the gospel "whether by life or by death" (v. 20). The Holy Spirit is the Comforter promised by the Risen Christ and the power source by which Paul will not be shamed and by which Jesus will be honored. Paul is confident that the prayers of the people will be answered and give Paul an even fuller measure of the Holy Spirit. His own faith, these prayers, and the presence of the Spirit will deliver him to eternity with the affirmation that he did his best for the glory of God. This is a joyful victory to be sure.

Hopeful Living

How can one live hopefully in the face of such hopelessness? How can one live joyfully in the face of such doom? Paul claims this joyful living through the Spirit of Christ. Paul found himself in a "no-lose" situation.

However, we should not be quick to "overspiritualize" Paul's faith. He is certainly a spiritual giant, but when we read deeper into these verses, we realize the depth of his human nature. In verse 23, Paul gives us a clue to his emotional state: "I am hard pressed." Paul is joyful but struggling, confident yet waivering. He is struggling with his humanity and his eternity. So do you and I. In being honest with the Philippians about his faith, he is modeling his faithfulness for them even as he confesses his struggles.

Paul's life is firmly grounded in Christ, through Christ, and for Christ. If he continues to live, he will daily proclaim the salvation of Christ and the joy of Christ. This is as natural for Paul as breathing. Paul is not choosing death to escape life; he is choosing life in order to live confidently in Christ in the face of struggles. He does not fear life.

Neither does Paul fear death. He knows that in his physical death, the Spirit of Christ will take him to an even fuller spiritual life. His life is a blessing, but even greater blessings are coming. For Paul, "living is Christ and dying is gain" (v. 21). He's not between a rock and hard place; he's between good and even better!

Paul is confronted with two good solutions. He feels the pull to continue living in Christ. He also feels the tug of heaven calling him to eternal blessings and release. It seems that he is torn between the two options, even to the point of believing that he will remain alive and see the Philippian congregation again (vv. 25-26). Paul's desire is not to live merely for his own sake. He desires life so that his witness may continue to glorify Christ. Furthermore, he anticipates death not as an end but as a continuation into the glory of Christ.

Paul rejoices in this passage, declaring with confidence that there is no containing the saving power of Christ. Too often we think we are responsible for the results of the gospel. We take credit for them. But Paul makes clear in this section that the gospel is more powerful than Pharisees with a prosperity agenda. It is more powerful than preachers with wrong motives, misguided theologies, or larger-than-life egos. These individuals cannot stop the gospel of Jesus Christ. Nothing is more powerful than the living and saving gospel of Jesus Christ!

The Redeeming Message

The message is always more important that the motive. We worry too much about our abilities with regard to preaching and teaching. Some of you resisted teaching this study, thinking you were not good enough to share the truth of God. Some of you resisted going through this study, thinking you were not good enough to participate.

Paul knows with assurance that God can transform the messenger and even redeem the message. The Holy Spirit is a powerful translator of misguided teaching and misplaced motives. It is a strong redeeming presence in the midst of competitive congregations or egotistical proclaimers. Paul lives in confidence that the Spirit of Christ will transcend our human frailties and deliver each of us into salvation.

Sometimes we lack confidence. We worry too much about our humanity. We've seen how the church treats her servants. We've heard stories of martyrs of the faith. Few of us are willing to pay that price. We're sure we don't want to face prison, much less death, for the sake of the gospel. We are prone to ask, "How can God let someone like Paul suffer so harshly?" What we are really thinking is, "Would God let *me* suffer that harshly?"

We know that Paul, and even more so Jesus, were exemplary in their devotion to God. We know that we are not even close to living the examples they set for us. We shy away from living the gospel. We are timid in sharing our own witness. We dare not speak openly of our faith for fear of embarrassment. But Paul has modeled for us a "Christ confidence" that will not be silent, that will look death in the face and laugh. How does one claim this kind of confidence?

Paul lived with a joyful attitude. He realized that neither his critics nor his competitors could impede the gospel. He realized that neither differing theologies nor varying worship expressions would weaken the gospel. Paul's joy was in Christ. For him, the Spirit of Christ was bigger than worship wars, poor preaching, congregational divisions, or weak thoughts.

Paul also lived within his own confidence. Paul knew faith had to be personalized. Others cannot give us our faith. We have to *know* it and own it for ourselves. Too many of us wish someone else would figure it out for us and tell us how to live and what to believe. Yet this misplaces our faith and keeps us from owning it. To be effective, faith must be personal, lived, tested, and lived again. This is the key to joyful victory.

Paul admonishes us to pray without ceasing. We tend to make this too difficult. Pray as you inhale, pray as you exhale. Even as we have to breathe, we can pray. Pray as you take one step and as you take another step. As we are walking from one place to another, we can pray. Pray as you get out of bed each day and as you go to bed at night. Pray as you eat, as you drink, as you work, as you play.

Anne Lamott encourages us to pray too. "Here are the two best prayers I know; Help me, Help me, Help me! Thank you, thank you, thank you!" (Lamott, 82). This is another good model for us to pray without ceasing.

Paul would affirm these practices and prayers. Surely, with each breath he took, he was praying. Surely with each meal he was served, he was praying. I suspect he prayed a lot of "Help me, thank you!" kind of prayers. Even death, the last threat that the world holds over us, has been subdued and defeated. Paul eagerly anticipates the day when he will die and be released into a greater victory.

Finally, notice the pastoral care and concern from Paul (vv. 25-26). He does not make the Philippians feel guilty that they haven't attained this same spirituality. He has been honest in his own spiritual struggles and would encourage the same from the Philippians. He deeply desires that they continue their faith journey even as he is continuing his own. He is honest ("I am struggling!"), and he is faithful ("I know that I will remain, continue, and share with you."). The same is true for us today. We desire to continue growing in Christ, overcoming diversity, and coping with our struggles. (Help me, help me, help me!) We too are grateful for the blessings God has given us on our journeys. (Thank you, thank you, thank you!)

Life Lessons

1. Why does God bless us? Are our blessings equal to the depth of our faith? What does God desire of us in our faith journeys?

_____

_____

_____

_____

_____

_____

2. How have you experienced the miraculous presence of God in the midst of personal pain and struggle? What blessings emerged in this experience? What lessons did you learn? What happened to your faith during this time?

_____

_____

_____

_____

_____

_____

_____

3. There is evidence in this section that Paul was struggling, yet his joy and confidence override his mental and emotional struggle. How was Paul able to live with such joy and confidence? How can we?

_____

_____

_____

_____

_____

_____

_____

4. Paul was not worried about his competition. What was his attitude? Why? How can we adopt a similar attitude to move from competition to collaboration? How might God's Kingdom benefit from our collaboration with neighbor churches? Why don't we collaborate more?

_____

_____

_____

_____

_____

_____

_____

5. How did a sense of urgency affect Paul's ministry? Do we have a sense of urgency about our ministries? Why or why not?

_____

_____

_____

_____

_____

_____

_____

6. What keeps us from sharing the gospel with more enthusiasm and energy? What needs to happen for us to grow more comfortable in service and in witness?

_____

_____

_____

_____

_____

_____

_____

7. What difficulties are you aware of in your congregation? What would Paul say to you about these? How do we let our humanity get in the way of the holy?

_____

_____

_____

_____

_____

_____

_____

8. In v. 20, we see that Paul's primary concern in the issues swirling around him is his own behavior. He wants to speak boldly and with confidence to glorify Christ. What was his source of confidence? What is your main focus in the issues swirling around you? What is your source of confidence?

_____

_____

_____

_____

_____

_____

_____

9. What keeps you from living a life of joyful victory? What lifestyle changes do you need to implement? What changes do you need to make in your attitude?

_____

_____

_____

_____

_____

_____

_____

10. What does it mean to be "Christ confident"? How do we achieve this? What difference does this confidence bring to our lives?

_____

_____

_____

_____

_____

_____

_____

Joyful Unity

I have led two churches through an interim without a senior minister. This "interim" period between leaders is a time to regroup, reorient, and make a congregation ready for the next pastoral leader. There are mixed feelings in congregations going through this time. Some are excited by the opportunity for change, while others are scared by what the "new" pastor will do. Some are challenged to step up and help in the interim, and some are stubborn and dig in to maintain the status quo.

For many people in both churches I served, these were sad times filled with unknown outcomes and unspoken hopes. Most everyone prayed that the new pastor would be in place sooner rather than later. Without the leadership of a senior minister, many of the people seemed lethargic, wringing their hands and wishing for God to act quickly. Many of the people couldn't recognize the leadership of the staff ministers and deacons. Others in the congregation wouldn't accept that anyone other than a senior minister could lead. Many felt that their church was about to die and close. Probably, more time was spent wringing hands in worry than bowing heads in prayer.

For many other people, these were exhilarating and challenging times of personal and corporate growth. The staff ministers took on the ministry responsibilities of the senior minister and kept the church operating at full strength. They worked hard to grow a deeper unity among the congregations. In both churches, new ministries were started and functioned with excellence under lay leadership. For the group of folks who tried new ventures, there was a prevailing sense of excitement. The sentiment was, "We can't wait until we have our next pastor in place! But until then, we're going to work hard at getting our congregation ready." These groups knew that bowed heads did more for their church's future than "wrung hands"!

In both congregations, most people focused on the good work that was happening or that needed to happen. While some in the congregations couldn't admit that things were going well, most tried to continue the good work of the church while preparing for the next chapter of ministry. Some people simply couldn't get past the idea of not having a senior minister. But the churches as a whole faired well and were more than ready for a new challenge as the next senior minister arrived.

Sadly, too few of our churches are like the two congregations I served. Too many of them put total confidence and dependence upon the person in the role of the senior minister. That is not fair to the senior minister, to other staff ministers, or to the congregation. The life and work of the congregation should center on the priesthood of *all* believers in Christ. We are a congregational people. Putting too many expectations on one person or in one role severely limits the life and work of the church. While the Philippian congregation doesn't seem to have depended on any one person, they were certainly connected to Paul.

"Whether I Come or Not," 1:27

In this passage, the tone shifts a bit from pastoral closeness, putting distance between Paul and the Philippians. So far, in this letter of joy, Paul has sought to bridge the geographical distance between him and the Philippians with the intimacy of words. He has used his expressions to conjure up sweet memories, to emphasize strong relationships, and to instill confidence. The people are intimately bonded with him as their "senior minister." There is no doubt that the missionary who helped begin this work still functions in many ways as pastor.

Paul seems to brace himself and the congregation for disappointment. He begins with the phrase, ". . . whether I come and see you or am absent and hear about you" (1:27). Basically, he tells them, "Even though I love you, you cannot be too dependent on me." As Fred Craddock says, "Paul's presence or absence is not the determining factor in living out the gospel of Jesus Christ" (32). Paul is letting the church know of his hope to be with them again. He also is cautioning the congregation that his hope and God's plan may not be the same.

Sessions with Philippians

I'm impressed with the honesty and sincere care Paul has for this congregation. He puts professional distance between them. His profession is pastor! Here we see the pastoral mindset at its best: this pastor cares for his congregation. In many ways, he is letting the congregation know that he loves them and cares for them. Yet he is also assuring them that they don't need his presence among them to be effective ministers.

Many of our churches would do well to hear this word today. Just as Paul was not the determining factor for the Philippian congregation, neither is your senior minister for your congregation. We are *all* called to be the church, the community of believers in a particular place. Regardless of whether your church currently has a senior minister, you and your congregation are not excused from doing the work of God's Kingdom.

Paul is clear about this to the Philippians. He is equally clear to us today!

Community Conduct, 1:27-30

Having distanced himself from the congregation, Paul now challenges the Philippians to live boldly in their community. This is a call to the intentional lifestyle of a disciple. To live with discipline and intentionality is to live a life "worthy" of the gospel. This was a huge challenge. The gospel, the good news of Jesus Christ, was still in the formative stages. There was no "gospel" in hard copy. There was no manual in print on how to be a church or a Christian. The gospel of Jesus Christ was emotional, relational, and spiritual. The gospel was loosely defined at this point. The call to live worthily of the gospel was a call to discipleship.

The Christian community of Paul's day was small and somewhat isolated from society. Many of the believers would have forsaken their family and friends to become part of the congregation. While most tried to blend their Christian faith with their Jewish heritage, this would not have been easy. Their family and friends outside the new faith would see this blending as a rejection of the Jewish faith. The believers would have been rejected by those closest to them. This would have been confusing to the Philippian Christians and certainly painful.

Paul's call to intentionality was a challenge indeed. The church would have to struggle together to achieve unity. It would have to define itself in the context of its own faith, not in the response to opponents or culture. There were no governing bodies or judicatories to guide the formation of churches. There were no guidelines or policy manuals for the "care and feeding" of a congregation. To live a life "worthy" of the gospel would be a serious challenge. Most of the believers were "making it up" as they lived each day.

Believers faced opposition from all sides—from family, from friends, from Roman officials, and from Jewish leaders. While we don't know exactly who the Philippians' opponents were, we know Paul's advice to the believers. Standing firm in the faith is the best response. (See 2 Cor 2:15-16 and Matt 5:14ff.)

The ability to live well in the face of opposition is a powerful witness. For the Christian community, overcoming the opposition of the wicked has always been a goal. Many of us are quick to pass judgment on those who are harsh to us. Many of us are "Old Testament" believers, claiming an eye for an eye and praying for God's retribution. Others claim to be "New Testament" believers, claiming the grace of God and praying for peaceful solutions. Regardless of where one might land concerning divine punishment, we all are sure that God needs to punish the offenders. We have no say, however, in how God deals with the wicked. We have a say only in our own behavior.

Paul calls the Philippians to live in a manner worthy of the gospel (v. 27). The Philippians would have to live as examples to fellow Christians and beyond. Yes, they would live as examples to one another. But, they would also live as examples to their opponents (v. 28).

Paul is probably writing from Rome, the heart of the Empire. He is writing to his beloved Philippians, a colony of Rome. The Philippians were part of the kingdom of God and the empire of Caesar. The Empire would expect them to be loyal to Caesar. Their opponents would expect behavior to the contrary. Paul stresses that believers must act with intentionality and with dignity appropriate to Rome and to Jesus. Paul does not want a violent uprising from this congregation. He expects intentional worthy living.

Paul expects that a manner "worthy" of the gospel would combine worthy Roman obedience *and* committed Christian living, loving one's opponents.

This is a calling from hierarchy to priority. Being a citizen of Rome was certainly an elevated position. There was power and privilege in being a Roman. However, being a follower of Christ, a "citizen of heaven," shifts the priority of life. No longer can one behave with power and privilege. Rather, the priority of the

Christian is to represent Christ, not Rome. No matter what happens in your faith, stand firm in Christ.

Suffering is part of faith. Struggle is part of faith. For too many, retreating and falling away are parts of faith. There are too many believers around the world who are suffering and struggling as they seek to represent their faith. And there are far too many who are abandoning the church and their faith altogether.

Even more than suffering and struggling, standing firm is part of faith. The church is not to hide its "light under a basket" (Matt 5:14ff.). The church is not to run from opposition (Matt 5:38ff.). The church is to stand firm, love enemies, and pray for those who are hurtful (Luke 6:27ff.).

In difficult times, believers have an opportunity to give a witness "worthy" of the gospel. As Christians stand firm in the face of opposition, they give a witness of strength and unity. They let the world know that they are unashamed of the gospel. For Paul, the opportunity to stand firm and to share a strong witness is a gift to the Philippian congregation.

Rarely do we think of facing opposition as a gift. Even more rarely do we embrace struggle as a blessing from God. But Paul encourages this congregation to hear his words and take them to heart, identifying with his own struggle. He invites the Philippians to make sense of their suffering through what they know of his. Finally, he encourages them to live in grace and give a witness as he is doing. Living a life worthy of the gospel means standing firm in our faith and living in the grace of Jesus Christ. The faithful may still be young and growing. The congregation may still be finding its way. The "gospel" may still be in development. But living a life worthy of the gospel means standing in the grace and strength of Jesus.

Congregational Conduct, 2:1-11

Stress can take a toll on congregational life. The challenge of standing firm often produces fissures in the fellowship. Too often, we let daily issues interfere with living worthily for the sake of the gospel. We simply become consumers of "religious" goods and services with no thought of congregational unity. We grow mean-spirited and selfish, developing tunnel vision about the needs of the congregation. Paul knows the human spirit. He knows that the opponents to the church at Philippi will try to erode their unity and commitment to the gospel.

Paul gives them a fourfold call to stand firm (v. 2). First, he calls them to stand firm being of the same mind. The congregation will have to know and adhere to the core values that brought them together. The founding principles would certainly be known by Paul and the founding members, perhaps the "bishops and deacons" of Philippians 1:1. Standing firm in the core values and founding beliefs would keep the church focused on their main ministries.

He also calls them to stand firm by having the same love. This would, of course, be the love of Jesus. As the Philippians live out of the love of Jesus, they live in a manner worthy of the gospel (v. 27). Certainly, living in the "same love" would not be easy when Roman soldiers are persecuting them and their Jewish families are rejecting them.

Standing firm also includes having the same spirit. The spirit of Christianity is the spirit of Jesus, empowered by the Holy Spirit. How easy it would be to be distracted and to live in the spirit of their own power and their own desires. As we think in similar ways, we hold similar core values. As we love in similar ways empowered by Christ, we respond in kindness to our neighbors. As we think and love, we are guided by the same spirit. This spirit of Jesus Christ unites us in service and in love, in worship and in praise.

Finally, standing firm urges the congregation to have the same purpose. What is this purpose? The call is to be the presence of Christ to one another, to their community, even to their world. Paul is letting the prison guard in Rome know of their witness and ministry. Paul implores the congregation to live in unity and in community.

He further calls the congregation to a stance of personal humility. He calls for a spirit of servanthood, one to another, that will focus more on serving and less on consuming. He calls for unity over selfishness. The bottom line for these verses is that Paul calls the congregation to be the presence of Christ to one another, to be the presence of Christ in their community, even as they are being the presence of Christ to Paul.

If the congregation is going to stand strong in their endeavors, there will have to be mutual encouragement among the members. Paul would have known of the strength of this fellowship. He certainly would have known of personal discouragement, his own and in the congregation. He knows (as he has already said) that the prayers of this church have carried him through some of his darkest days. He calls the church to use this same energy and faithfulness for lifting up one another. He knows that soon he will not be able to encourage them. He, therefore, is teaching them, admonishing them, to love one another. Loving one another, praying for one another will keep them firm in unity of mind, of ministry, of purpose.

He also tells the church to stand strong because of their unity in the Holy Spirit. The Spirit is the great Comforter binding them into the goodness of God's love and binding them into the goodness of their love for one another. The Spirit of God enables them (and us) to live the gospel "worthily." Paul knows that in prayer and faithfulness, the fellowship of the congregation can find stability, strength, and unity.

Paul is not questioning the faith or the dedication of the Philippians; he is acting as a worried pastor. He affirms them for their goodness and their faithfulness and pleads with them to stay strong. He knows human nature all too well! He doesn't point to their negatives; he doesn't put unnecessary guilt on them. He simply and honestly reminds them to be faithful and to stay faithful. If they are faithful, they will stay united in their calling as Christians and as a congregation. He seems to be saying, "Remember your calling. Remember why we formed as a congregation."

There is evidently some problem already arising in the church. Paul is trying to use his personal bond with the Philippians to encourage them to unity. Paul lets them know that his joy will only be completed as they stay faithful. His prayers will have been answered and his joy will overflow as they live worthily in the gospel.

Paul reminds the church of the values that brought them together. He reminds them of their purpose as a congregation. There is in this congregation a strength of faith to sustain them and help them grow even stronger. There is at play in the Philippian congregation a set of core values that formed them and has guided them. These core values are what has unified them in the past, what will keep them strong in the days to come. The fact that Paul speaks to this at all may indicate that some inside the church and, for sure, outside the church have called these values into question. Paul encourages unity, selflessness, and humility.

He adds an exclamation point with the inclusion of Jesus as their model. The hymn in vv. 6-11, rich in praise of God in Christ, was likely familiar to the Philippian congregation. Our congregations are filled with our hymns of praise for God's grace. Your congregation certainly has its "Greatest Hits list" that may include hymns like "Amazing Grace," "The Old Rugged Cross," "Holy, Holy, Holy," and "How Great Thou Art." You may sing the "Doxology" together every Sunday. Perhaps you always sing "Silent Night" on Christmas Eve. Sound familiar?

These verses are probably a common Philippian hymn. Some scholars think Paul is composing a hymn for the church. Some think he is "borrowing" a hymn to bring particular emphasis to his letter. But all scholars agree that this was probably a hymn that was beloved and integral to congregational life.

The hymn emphasizes the need for Jesus' influence on them. This church needs praise rather than pettiness. This church needs service and obedience to the spirit of Jesus rather than empty memorization and recitation of religious facts. To live worthily in the gospel is to live as Christ lived! That's what the Philippian church needs and what we need today!

Paul is never against individual responsibility. To the contrary, he repeatedly calls us to be responsible for our own salvation experience and Christlikeness. (See Gal 6:4-5 and Phil 2:12.) However, individual faith contributes to the higher calling of congregational unity. The Philippians need to grasp this point, and so do we today.

The Christian has two great honors: to believe in Christ and to suffer for the sake of Christ (Phil 1:29-30; Stagg, 192ff). The honor to believe is a direct result of the sacrifice of Jesus Christ and the loving grace of God. Many of us live in this honor daily and are to God grateful for it.

The honor to suffer for the sake of Christ comes with maturity. To suffer means that we struggle against the forces of the world that continually pull us away from our faith. Paul is certainly struggling, and he calls the Philippian church to do the same. For many in this congregation (and in our congregations), perhaps the biggest challenge of suffering for the sake of Christ is surrendering our individuality and selfish desires for the greater good of the congregation. We cannot sing the great hymn "I Surrender All" and then demand our own way. We cannot sing "How Great Thou Art" and live like "I" am the center of the universe.

The way to live a life worthy of the gospel becomes clearer as Paul continues to clarify his pastoral thoughts. The life worthy of the gospel sings hymns of praise. The life worthy of the gospel stands firm in the face of opposition. The life worthy of the gospel builds unity.

Christian Conduct, 2:12-13

So then, how are we to live? First and foremost, we are to live on bended knee. In humbling ourselves to the higher calling of Christ Jesus, we admit that a higher power than our own is at work in the world. This call to humility (and submission to Christ) keeps us focused more on living congregationally and less on living individually. Paul has reminded the Philippians that they already have the mind of Christ in them (2:5). Now he calls them to live humbly, putting into practice what they already know. They are encouraged to work out in the life of the congregation what is already evident in their individual lives.

Secondly, Paul reminds the congregation that we not only live with humility but we also live confessionally. Working out one's salvation with fear and trembling means daily confessing the lordship of Christ. This humble and confessional attitude will keep us focused on Christ. One can hardly be self-centered when on bended knee with a confessional attitude.

This bended-knee, confessional intentionality keeps us surrendering to Christ daily and living in awe and appreciation. Paul is not calling us to be afraid in our faith or to be fearful of God. Paul calls us to servanthood. This is a daily practice of putting on the mind of Christ and living carefully and prayerfully.

"Fear and trembling" is an attitude that leads to a lifestyle of service, which is pleasing to God. This is neither a call to cowardice nor a call to doubt. This is a call to reverence and confidence. "Fear and trembling" keeps us from an arrogant self-confidence and leads to a humble Christ confidence. Paul challenges the congregation to continually "lean in" to their salvation, living to the fullest in Christ. Living in "fear and trembling" is one more way to live a life worthy of the gospel.

This "fear and trembling" is also a reminder that, while God is at work in them and with them, God is still bigger than them. God is God! There is no familiarity with the Divine. God is not one of us. When we begin to believe we know the mind of God, trouble ensues. When we live in the arrogance of thinking we know what God knows, we soon discover how little we actually know. The One who grants the gift of eternal life is not one of us! Paul warns the congregation to stay humble and to live with awe and humility rather than arrogance and certainty.

In these days of technological sophistication, medical miracles, and amazing human accomplishments, we would do well to realize that God is the giver of good gifts. In the midst of such wonderful advancements in the world, let us not forget that God is the author and finisher of our lives. My "smart phone" is a wonderful tool. My wide-screen, high-definition television is a marvelous entertainment and information center. My laptop computer keeps me connected to friends all around the world.

But my salvation, the assurance of God's love for me in Christ Jesus, is my most prized possession. I prayerfully start each day with "fear and trembling" in hopes that I will be worthy of living for Christ and trying to be the presence of Christ to those on my path. How about you?

Life Lessons

1. The life and work of the congregation centers on the reality of the priesthood of all believers in Christ. How are you serving as a priest among the people in your congregation? What is your calling to service? What do you need from your congregation in order to be equipped for service?

_____

_____

_____

_____

_____

_____

_____

2. "The ability to live well in the face of opposition is a powerful witness." Do you agree or disagree with this statement? How does one "stand firm" in their faith? What does it mean for YOU to live the gift of opposition in your faith?

_____

_____

_____

_____

_____

_____

_____

3. Paul makes it clear that the Philippians already have the mind of Christ in them. He urges them to claim this, to realize it, and to live it—to become more of who they already are. How can we do this today? What is the difference between "claiming" a gift and "realizing" a gift? What do you need to become more of who you already are in Christ?

_____

_____

_____

_____

_____

_____

_____

4. What is your favorite hymn? How does praise bring us closer to God? Give us strength? Help us live worthily? What is the role of worship in your everyday life?

_____

_____

_____

_____

_____

_____

_____

5. A set of core values formed and guided the Philippian congregation. What are the core values of your congregation? How have these values guided your congregation in days of testing? How do these core values guide you to stay strong as an individual believer?

_____

_____

_____

_____

_____

_____

_____

6. What is the purpose of your individual call to faith? How can we keep our individuality in Christ from being the sole purpose of our faith? What is God calling you to do in your congregation? What is God calling you to do in the world?

_____

_____

_____

_____

_____

_____

_____

7. What are your three most prized possessions? How do you guard against consumerism? How are you working out your salvation with fear and trembling?

_____

_____

_____

_____

_____

_____

_____

8. What are some indicators that God is still at work in you and with you? How do you live with humility and in a spirit of confession?

_____

_____

_____

_____

_____

_____

_____

9. Who needs you to be the presence of Christ to them today? How will you know? What will you do?

_____

_____

_____

_____

_____

_____

_____

Joyful Models

Philippians 2:14-30

Would you rather be involved in "doing" or "being"? In these verses, Paul advises the congregation on how to be in Christ—to be joyful children of God. This is not an easy task for any of us. Most of us would rather *do* something than simply *be*. If someone will just tell me what to do, I'll be glad to do it. When I see something that needs doing, I respond to the needs. We are all good at doing things; just look at our calendars and our checkbooks.

Being is another subject altogether. Most of us even ask the question from a "doing" perspective, "What do I have to do to just be?"

Part of my work involves leading prayer retreats for ministers and church leaders. We spend time praying and worshiping together. We get to know one another better and share our stories of faith. We learn about the practices of prayer and spiritual disciplines. We spend a lot of time looking at resources and talking about how to *do* prayer work in the church.

We also spend a significant amount of time in silence, contemplating the vastness of God and our place in God's plan. The main goal of these retreats is to *be* with God. We spend time in silence to *be* silent. We encourage participants to do nothing. We invite participants simply to be with God.

Many participants resist this. They want to *do*. They want to talk and visit and dialogue and debate. They want to pray and worship out loud. They want to fellowship and share. They don't want to be silent!

But our retreat model involves a lot of silence. More than half of the three-day experience is spent in silence, listening to God and for God. We even eat one meal in silence. (You'd be surprised how loud mashed potatoes can sound when there is no other noise in the dining hall!) At the conclusion of worship each evening until the next morning, there is silence.

There are no televisions, cell phones, or iPods. We encourage being with God and self. Yet being with God and only our thoughts is not easy. Focusing all one's attention on the Spirit of God and discerning who God is and how one fits into God's plan is challenging. Remarkably, by the end of the three-day retreat, most of our participants want to stay another day or two. Being with God is an amazing experience (cf. Matt 17).

There is always a delicate balance of living between works and grace, between doing and being. Paul has shared clearly with the Philippians that they are to work out their salvation with fear and trembling. He has talked much about doing. He has given instructions on what to do, how to do, and the attitude with which to do. Now he moves to the challenge of "being," sharing poignant pictures of joy.

Be Like Joyful Children, 2:14-18

Simply doing is not enough; doing all things in the right way with the right attitude is the challenge. Philippians is a letter about responding to this "right" challenge. Paul speaks to the "doing" part of church and the "doing" part of faith in these verses.

Verses 12-16 are full of the admonition to *work*, to *do*! Paul tells the congregation to obey and work out their own salvation (v. 12). He reminds them that God is at work (v. 13). Paul emphasizes that he has been working, that they are to be working, and that God is working. Work is good, work is needed, and work is ordained by God.

When studying Philippians, however, the danger exists that the reader will emerge with a motivation to work, work, work. There is certainly always work to do, a ministry to share, and another visit to make. Yet, if one does not care for one's spirit, the energy to engage will soon disappear, attitudes will sour, and spirits will sag. "Soul care" is perhaps the most difficult discipline to practice. Paul reminds the congregation that they are to work not for his affirmation, not for their own accomplishment, but for the good pleasure of God (v. 13).

Paul shifts from words about fear and trembling to words about a child (v. 15). They are to "be like children," but not just any children—"children of God." What a wonderful model! Children are filled with innocence and energy. They naturally seek God and seek to represent God to the world. I love it when children run down the aisles for the children's sermon during worship. I love Vacation Bible School and the energy of the children. I love baptizing children and watching them "dog paddle" out of the baptistery. They come with no pretense. They come with no attitude. They are innocent and blameless and fun. Paul calls us all to live this way.

The Philippian congregation is too sophisticated to become children. They are struggling with grumbling, debate, and strained relationships. Their negative attitudes are taking a toll. Paul calls the adult members to stop arguing about the faith and to live it joyfully and innocently, as children of God.

Too often, adults want to make the church a place for theological debate. Too often, adults would rather gossip (even when sharing prayer requests). Too often, adults grumble about our Christian witness or are too lazy to participate in ministry opportunities. We have allowed these negative attitudes to exist in our churches. We have tolerated lazy, grumbling, and negative people.

A church member once wildly exclaimed to me, "I don't have to come to this church, you know. I pass a lot of churches to get to this one!"

I wanted to reply, "Well, I wish you had stopped at one of them instead of bringing your mean spirit to our church." Instead, I smiled and told her how much we appreciated her dedication to our church. Adults have a way of being negative and mean-spirited.

But not children! Children live into the moment with joy and energy. Children don't dilute the faith but embrace it wholeheartedly. Children don't grumble about ministry or debate their faith. Children are sometimes brutally honest, but they are rarely cold and calculating. They are rarely mean spirited. Even their anger is usually short lived.

The Philippians are called to hear the words of Jesus in John 17:15, "to be in the world but not of the world." Children instinctively understand the difference. Most adults have to work at it!

The joyful Christian lives without regret. Living life to the fullest is freeing. My wife and I were coming home from dinner, talking about how life has taken us down twists and turns. I said to her, "I wouldn't change anything. I have no regrets about how we've lived our lives. The mistakes we've made and the pain we've caused have served to make us more aware, made us stronger, drawn us closer. Life is too short at this point to worry about the things we can't change!"

I'm not sure if this is childish or childlike, but I hope it is an attempt to embrace my inner child. Living life to the fullest is freeing. Living in innocence and without blemish is the goal. None of us can achieve this, but it is a worthy target to shoot for.

Be Like Paul, 2:14-18

We have all fallen short, no doubt. My sins do grieve me, but worry and regret suck the life out of me if I'm not careful. As the bumper sticker states, "Christians aren't perfect, just forgiven!"

Continually striving to live with innocence and without blemish is the best approach. Paul uses himself as a role model of how to live as a "child of God." He urges the congregation to be blameless and live boldly. There is no doubt that Paul claims this forgiveness as the leader of this missionary congregation. He does not claim perfection for himself or for the Philippians. Volumes have been written on the leadership and theology of Paul. For this study, it is enough to understand that Paul puts himself forward as a model of how to be a faithful Christian. He does this not out of arrogance but out of his love for the people. They heard him as people who knew him personally. We can't do this, but we can be sure that he is motivated out of love for them rather than his ego.

He challenges the congregation to yearn for joyful innocence (see Phil 3:14). The Philippians find themselves in a world gone wrong. They see perverse behavior, crooked business people, and darkness in their own hearts. The congregation is to be light in the darkness, blameless in the perversity, and innocent in the crooked places. The call from their spiritual hero is to be joyful children of light, following the model Paul learned from Jesus.

The same darkness, perverse behaviors, and crooked places exist today. Pick up the newspaper or go to your favorite Internet news page. Paul beckons us today as he did his beloved Philippians. The economy is failing. Government is dealing every day with another scandal. World societies are rioting and looting. The same darkness that Paul battled is also threatening our faith. Paul challenged the Philippian congregation to let Christ live in them and through them. Perhaps Paul issues the same challenge to us today.

Paul sets his model of joy before us now to become light, blameless and innocent. The goal is to live as Christ, and Paul's own life is one example that he would offer to us. But, true to his leadership, he is not the only role model.

Be Like Timothy, 2:19-24

Paul is writing about himself in these passages. However, he does not hold himself up as the only role model. Timothy is also a fitting and experienced leader. He is certainly known by the Philippians (1 Cor 4:17-19; Acts 16:1-5). Paul is Timothy's "father in ministry." Timothy is special; Paul trusts him, and he is familiar to the Philippian church. He is a believer worth imitating.

Paul knows the Philippians will receive Timothy as if they were receiving Paul himself. Timothy's role is to go to them to bring good news and cheer to the congregation. Paul expects Timothy to bring a model of joy to the Philippians amid their struggles. In turn, Timothy can return to Paul telling him how the Philippians embraced him and lived into the joy of Christ. Timothy will not come to find good cheer; he will come to bring it in hopes that the Philippian congregation can heal. Paul sends out the good news of Jesus through Timothy, hoping that it will not return to him void but rather be multiplied (see Eccl 11:1ff). Paul is in prison. He faces death. He needs a lift from this beloved congregation. Who better to take the good news to the Philippians and to bring a report of joy than Timothy?

Timothy is not in this for himself. His ego is not tied up in his ministry. Timothy is devoted to the calling of Christ through the ministry of Paul. He discovered joyful living from Paul's ministry to him, and he still seeks to grow closer to Christ by serving his mentor faithfully. Timothy is living out the joy of his salvation by serving his ministerial father, his eternal Lord, and his Heavenly Parent.

His devotion is rewarded. Paul refers to him as his partner, his equal in ministry and faithfulness. What a tremendous affirmation of one who began as a young boy in the service of Paul! Paul has other associates who serve and share. However, Paul knows no one else who lives in the presence of Christ as Timothy does.

The fact that Paul can rely so heavily on Timothy is a tribute to his son in ministry. However, it is also a tribute to Paul's personal security. He is the leader of this ministry, but he is secure enough to commend others to do the work he wishes to do. Timothy is the successor to the leadership role of Paul. Those with less confidence would have looked at their successor as a rival. Timothy's growth, though, is a tribute both to Paul and to Jesus. Paul is filled with joy because of Timothy, and Timothy is filled with joy because of Paul. Both are filled with joy because of Christ Jesus.

My own ministerial "father," Jack, began as my hero, seemingly unapproachable and all knowing. The day I got to "sit" under his teaching was a day of great joy. As I introduced myself to him afterward, he shared his business card, his direct phone number, and his friendship. He soon became my mentor. Through my years of listening to his every word, I grew. Under his gentle guidance, my ministry began to form.

Years later, he invited me to come to his church and teach his Sunday school teachers. He introduced me as a leader in Christian Education and someone he was proud to share with his church leaders. He elevated me to the level of his colleague. I beamed with pride. Along the way, we shared together, we laughed together, and we cried together. We grew a special friendship that has lasted longer than his life. He lives on in my memory and in my tributes to him.

I understand Timothy's joy at being blessed by Paul. Timothy's story has been replicated in relationship after relationship in ministry. I'm grateful for Jack, my hero, mentor, colleague, and friend. Many of us have been like Timothy along the way. Many of us are also like Paul, finding gifted young leaders and sharing with them in their ministry journeys.

As special as my friend has been in my life and ministry, he made it clear that our relationship was never about him. The foundation of our friendship existed because of Christ. He never let me forget that my journey was one of faith and that the source for my joy was Jesus. Paul would agree. By sending Timothy, he is setting Timothy up as a role model who exemplifies Paul's leadership but always keeps Christ Jesus at the forefront!

Be Like Epaphroditus, 2:25-30

You may have never noticed this servant. He is only mentioned in Philippians 2:25-30. He was probably a pagan who was converted; his name originates from the name of the Greek goddess Aphrodite. Epaphroditus is from Philippi. Paul is now sending him back home, but he returns to the church as more than the messenger they earlier sent to Paul. He returns with Paul's commendation as "brother, fellow worker, and fellow soldier." This is high praise from Paul.

Epaphroditus has been physically sick and also distressed over the difficulties among the Philippian church. He was also in danger at some point, risking his life for the gospel. this servant risked it all for the ongoing work of the ministry. He is quite the role model!

Epaphroditus persevered in the midst of sickness. He continued in service even though he was near death. He risked his life for the ministry. His faithfulness is stellar, and Paul lifts him up as an example to the Philippians. Paul seems to have deeper motivations, however, than just affirming his friend.

The implication is that if Epaphroditus can endure his travails for the sake of the gospel, then surely the Philippians can set aside their pettiness and selfishness. The Philippians are to receive Epaphroditus with honor and joy. How could a congregation rejoice at the faithfulness of one of their own and still continue petty quarrels?

But having Epaphroditus return home did present a quandary. The Philippians had sent him to care for Paul. They had sent him to engage in ministry with their beloved missionary pastor. For Paul to send Epaphroditus home might communicate the wrong signal. Some might consider Epaphroditus to be a quitter in the face of hard times. Others might think Paul was not helped by Epaphroditus and was sending him home because he was unhelpful.

To avoid any misunderstanding, Paul spells it out clearly. This man has been a devoted friend to Paul and a valued member of his missionary force. To receive him with anything less than a hero's welcome would not only dishonor Epaphroditus but also dishonor Paul. Paul would add, parenthetically, that it would dishonor Christ. Epaphroditus is sent home as an affirmation for himself and the Philippian congregation. Paul speaks boldly to squelch any critical word that might be raised against this faithful friend and valuable missionary partner.

Final Thoughts

Paul yearns for spiritual growth and health to return with a passion to the Philippian church. He wants deeply for the joy of their salvation to become more evident. He holds himself up as a model to which they can aspire.

This passage is a beautiful testimony to the intimate relationship Paul has with this congregation. He is in prison, facing death, awaiting some decision about his own welfare. Most of us would hold firmly to trusted friends and want them with us.

Not so with Paul. He sends his two most trusted friends away, back to Philippi. He holds up Timothy as a role model. He holds up Epaphroditus as an equally credible role model. Paul is able to give up his closest friends for the sake of the congregation.

Paul is writing a personal letter to a congregation who knows him and who is known by him. His use of personal examples and transparency only magnifies his love for this congregation. While we can't relate to Paul's challenges on a deep personal basis, we can relate to the moral fiber of which he speaks. Our challenge is similar to that of the Philippian church. We are to revive the joy of Christ in one another and to become more of who we already are in Christ Jesus.

Life Lessons

1. What was your favorite game as a child? What was your favorite television program as a child? What was your favorite childhood pet? What did you want to be when you grew up? Who was a role model for you when you were a child? What did each of these teach you about growing up?

_____

_____

_____

_____

_____

_____

2. What is the role of a light? What are the differences between a car headlight and a candle? What are the similarities? What kind of light does your faith represent today? Are you comfortable with that kind of light? What kind of light do you aspire to become?

_____

_____

_____

_____

_____

_____

_____

3. Are you more childish or childlike? Why? How can you move closer into childlikeness? What is the most fun you've ever had at church? What did that event teach you about the joy of being a Christian?

_____

_____

_____

_____

_____

_____

_____

4. What darkness in our world would you most like to illuminate? Why this darkness? What is the root of this darkness? How can you and your church begin to eradicate it? What needs to happen for you to allow Christ to live more in you and through you?

_____

_____

_____

_____

_____

_____

_____

5. What regrets in your life do you need to turn loose? What darkness and guilt is sucking the life out of you? How would Paul bless you in turning loose of these shortcomings? Perhaps, write prayers of blessing and forgiveness and pray these together.

_____

_____

_____

_____

_____

_____

_____

Joyful Models

6. What character traits does Paul model for us? What character traits does Timothy model for us? What character traits does Epaphroditus model for us? To which of these three do you relate the most? Why?

_____

_____

_____

_____

_____

_____

_____

7. What sacrifices have you made for the cause of the gospel? How have these experiences formed you spiritually? How might these be used as examples to other Christians?

_____

_____

_____

_____

_____

_____

_____

8. What would spiritual growth and health look like to Paul? What would these look like in your church? How can you be a vessel of redemption for your church in the way Epaphroditus was to the Philippians?

_____

_____

_____

_____

_____

_____

_____

9. Who are your role models for living a joyful adult life? How have they influenced your life? What have they taught you about living with joy? Who needs for you to be a role model for them? What changes do you need to make to become more of a role model?

_____

_____

_____

_____

_____

_____

_____

6 Joyful Living

Philippians 3:1–4:9

The whole world changed on September 11, 2001. Perhaps you watched in horror (or saw the video replays) of that fateful day in American history. No one in their wildest dreams thought terrorists would ever strike on our soil. As the Twin Towers fell, so did our hope and trust.

Prior to September 11, 2001, we were hopeful, trusting, and probably a bit naïve. Now we live in a world filled with fear and anxiety. You can almost feel the fear. Most advertising is geared to alleviate it. Advertisers of everything from teenage acne products to car batteries pitch their commercials to speak to our fear.

In the past decade, varied scares have raised serious questions. Is my pantry stocked for the Y2K crash? If I get the H1N1 vaccine, can I still eat pork? Where can I safely keep money since the economy is at its worst since the Great Depression? How can we ever eat shrimp from the Gulf Coast again after the BP oil spill? How will we ever drive our cars with gasoline at over five dollars a gallon? And what about the killer bees coming our way? The toxins in every morsel of fast food?

We live in a time when we are warned not to go outside without sunscreen, not to buy anything online, and not to eat too much chocolate or drink too many diet drinks. No matter how hungry we may be, under no circumstances should we eat fast food. Fear warns us of clogged arteries and elevated sodium levels with every burger or chicken sandwich. Even the medicines we take to keep us healthy come with warnings of side effects worse than the cause we seek to cure. Fear is rampant.

Such messages of fear rarely pan out. They get strong publicity and bring extra cash to those who claim to sell something that counteracts the fear. But the people who give these messages make me angry. They play on our anxieties instead of helping us cope in the chaos.

My wife and I have instilled two questions in our daughters to combat their anxieties: (1) What blessings are you receiving? (2) What positive lessons are you learning? This approach to examining life seems to put a more positive spin on the world.

In this mindset, even bad situations come with blessings. Even bad situations can teach us positive lessons about life. This approach seems more joyful than living in fear and anxiety. As we approach life from a more positive stance, we come to understand that most of our fears and worries never happen. These two questions let us live with expectations of blessings rather than fear, of hope rather than doubt. These two questions begin to get at what Paul is trying to say to his beloved Philippians (and to us).

We each have choices. One can choose to live in fear and anxiety, or one can choose to be proactive. One can choose to give in to the chaos and worry, or one can choose to rejoice in Christ. The choice is ours. No matter which approach we take, we must ask two questions: What are the blessings and what are the lessons?

Perhaps we should go a step further with one more question: How can we rejoice daily in these blessings and lessons?

Live Joyfully, 3:1-11

The first eleven verses of chapter 3 are something like a roller coaster ride. Paul twists and turns his way around these verses, catching his breath, slowing down, lurching at his critics, and ending up hoping for resurrection. He says a mouthful in these verses, but the bottom line is that we "live joyfully" no matter what happens.

Joy, not fear, is the way to life. Joy belongs to those on the pathway of discipleship. This congregation will likely hear Paul's letter read several times. He wants to be certain that they hear his encouragement to rejoice no matter what happens. He wants them to hear, individually and congregationally, that joy must undergird the life of a disciple.

He even says that he is not afraid of continually repeating this message. He is not afraid of writing the same things to them. This may mean he has sent them other letters in the past. This may mean that even in the body of this letter, he is repeating his message of joy. Regardless of what may lie beneath the words, Paul is clear about the message: "Rejoice always!" Joy is at the heart of discipleship.

Grumbling, false beliefs, and dissension keep us from growing as disciples. Paul addresses this in v. 2: "Beware the dogs, the evil doers, and those who mutilate the flesh." He knows that not everyone lives with joy and that the Christian life is challenging. But he also lives with an intense love for this congregation. For him to speak so strongly about the dangers to the church grabs the attention of the hearers. Paul yells, "Beware!" He warns against the "dogs" that would rob the Philippians of their joy.

Paul is pointing out places where the Philippians can expect spiritual attacks. Some of the believers at Philippi come from a Jewish background. Some are Gentile. For each group, what it means to be a follower of Christ is defined by differing sources of what it means to live a life of faith. The diversity within the congregation was likely a source of stress and dissension.

There are also false preachers among them. They are trying to distort Christianity and cause a rift between the Jewish and Gentile believers.

One group is preaching "circumcision" (those who mutilate the flesh) as the way to salvation. They brag about their own circumcisions. They exhort all males to undergo this ritual because it is needed for salvation. They stress the practice as a sign of true salvation and dedication to God. (Imagine adult males hearing this action as a necessary condition for being loved by God!)

This preaching is offensive to Paul's Christian faith and to his Jewish heritage. His name-calling emphasizes how repulsed he feels. His strong warning about these false preachers is given to grab the attention of the Philippians. He almost seems to shout a warning to his listeners.

Paul knows that salvation comes from the *grace* of God. He emphasizes this truth to the Philippians with passion and energy. He wants to ensure the attentiveness of his audience. At issue is whether the grace of God alone is sufficient for salvation. Paul battled this thought in other churches as well (see Rom 10:4-13 or Gal 2:1-5) and never backed down. God is sufficient in God's grace! This is the source for joyful living.

Others in Philippi are preaching deceptively to "win" Christians back to Judaism. They want to make Christianity seem legalistic and narrow. They want Judaism to seem more attractive and to make Jewish followers appear more blessed by God.

These preachers make circumcision and baptism a test of fellowship. They seek to relate all aspects of Christianity to legalistic tests.

Paul says, "No!" He emphatically declares that Christians are the true circumcised. He is adamant that Christians can be totally confident in the spirituality of Christ rather than in the ceremony of the flesh. Circumcision is not a condition of salvation. Faith is not a condition of ceremony. Paul is very clear that the only test of faith is belief. Salvation is not a gift based on one's circumcision, baptism, or any other "outward" sign or ceremony.

Some in Philippi are preaching that belief in Christ *plus* angels equals salvation (Col 2:8-23). Some preach that Christ *plus* Moses equals salvation (Rom 10:4-13). Some preach that Christ *plus* circumcision or baptism or other ceremonies equal salvation.

Christ plus anything else stirred Paul to fiery preaching. For Paul, God's grace makes us righteous. Christ *alone* equals salvation—nothing more, nothing less, nothing else. Preaching Christ *plus* anything else is false and even sinful.

We would do well to remember this when we put ceremony above belief and attach conditions to faith. We are called to live confidently in Christ. This means our faith is much more a priority than any ceremony or ritual. We do not receive redemption by circumcision, baptism, Communion, or any other activity or event.

These outward expressions of our faith in Christ are merely celebrations of our redeeming relationship with Christ. Whatever the celebration or ceremony, Paul makes it clear that our joy is in our relationship with God through Christ.

Hear the yearning of his soul in v. 10: "I want to know Christ . . . ." Paul yearns for an ever-deepening intimacy with Jesus so that he can live more obediently. He wants to grow deeper and deeper with Jesus so that he can live joyfully.

Paul yearns for growth in Christ! The desire of his heart is to grow more intimate with Christ He preaches that he will give up anything for a closer relationship with Christ. Paul has already given up quite a bit, but at the center of his faith is the desire to *live* as Christ. Living joyfully comes through an intimate relationship with Jesus. Living joyfully may be celebrated in ceremony, but it is certainly not dependent upon ceremony. The key to living joyfully is growing in Christ.

Grow Joyfully, 3:12-21

In order to achieve this depth of relationship with Christ, Paul preaches that we will have to grow. Some view growth as a negative process filled with changes against one's will. It brings fear and anxiety that threaten relationships and activities. Many of us resist growth for these reasons.

For Paul and many others, growth is a positive process based on hope rather than fear. Though it is filled with change, the change is positive and forms us more deeply. For Paul and others, growth offers the possibility of a deeper confidence in Christ that leads to joyful living.

Paul preaches that we will be resurrected even as Jesus was resurrected. He understands this resurrection to have benefits at death, but also in life. Knowing that we will be resurrected beckons us to keep growing. Christ's resurrection gives us power for living. We know that as we endure the challenges of this life, we are living like Christ. If Paul can learn and grow joyfully, even as a prisoner of Rome, we too can learn and grow joyfully.

Paul reminds them that he has not attained what he desires. He is striving, running, wrestling, and fighting to continue growing. Trusting God's grace and striving toward the resurrection do nothing to take away the struggles of daily living. But Paul knows that the adversities only make him stronger, make his faith grow deeper, and make his joy richer. For Paul there is no fear, no worry, and no anxiety—only joy.

Paul uses the illustration of a sprinter in a race. He is straining forward, leaning into the tape at the finish line. His eye is on the prize of resurrection. He is not looking at his feet or thinking about his stride; these have become second nature. He urges the Philippians to imitate his life. He encourages them to enter the race of life and strive with him toward the priority of living, growing in Christ, and deepening their joy.

Paul is not rejecting his roots of Judaism. He is not giving up his past and the memories of his earlier life. To the contrary, he is building upon them. The Philippians would know of his reputation as Pharisee and persecutor of believers. He does not deny these actions.

Memory is critical as we continue to grow in Christ. Paul accepts his "history" as part of his growth process. And he lets go of the things in his life that keep him from growing in the joy of

Joyful Living

Christ. He embraces his memories of the Philippians, which keep him alive and engaged. Even more important, he embraces the memories of his past, which keep him growing in the grace of God and straining forward.

The admonition from Paul the preacher is to follow his example. Paul preaches, "Imitate me and others who live according to the example you have in us." Not only does he continually emphasize joy, but he also emphasizes the models of himself, Timothy, Epaphroditus, and other leaders in the faith. Paul never preaches lofty ideas without giving practical application.

"Live joyfully, live in the way we have shown you," Paul says. "Listen to these words I keep repeating to you! Follow the example we are giving you. Do not be deceived into living with fear and anxiety. Live hopefully; live joyfully!"

Reconcile Joyfully, 4:1-3

Paul begins the fourth chapter by returning to the tension within the congregation. While he has spoken to this already, in these verses he gets personal. He gives names! It is bold preaching, but Paul invokes his pastoral privilege.

We don't know the issues swirling around these two women, Euodia and Syntyche, but we know that Paul is concerned enough to speak directly to them. Their argument is taking its toll on the congregation. Paul lets the women and the church know that he cannot tolerate this break in fellowship.

Negativity is robbing the Philippians of their joy in Christ. This dissension is in deep contrast to straining joyfully toward the prize of Christ. Paul calls the congregation "my joy and crown, beloved" to remind them again of how special they are to him. He is intimate enough with this congregation to relate to them endearingly. His intimacy also allows him to speak frankly about their bad behavior. While these two women may have thought their quarrel was private, Paul brings it into the open. Their breach of fellowship threatens the fellowship of the entire congregation.

We don't know these women. We don't know their argument. But just as Paul knew the danger of their dispute to the Philippian congregation, we know the toll dissension takes on the fellowship of *our* congregations. Paul appeals to them and to us to agree in the Lord, reconcile joyfully, and move on with the work.

Paul calls the congregation and perhaps one specified person ("true yokefellow") to be vessels of redemption to these two women.

They are good workers. They have been workers with Paul in the gospel. They have probably been on Paul's "missionary staff"! He is concerned that they get back on track, focused on the call of Christ rather than their individual differences.

To set aside their differences for the fellowship of the church and the sake of the gospel would bring joy to them and to Paul. Paul does not want to embarrass these women. He models the truth that leaders in the church will be held accountable. Leaders are not exempt from the values and goals of the congregation. Paul certainly makes this clear.

Additionally, Paul makes it clear that he expects the congregation to help these two women reconcile. Too often in church conflict, we bow our heads and avoid the issues. Too often, we don't engage the people who are the sources of the conflict. Paul expects the congregation to bring resolution to the problem and aid in redeeming this broken relationship. It is joyful reconciliation.

Paul does not call on the pastor of the church to resolve this issue. He does not call on the deacons of the church. He calls on the people of the church.

Paul gives a supreme compliment to the congregation. He believes they are capable of resolving the problem and helping these women. The congregation is actually more than capable; they are expected to help. The women's reconciliation and healing will bring joy to Paul and the congregation.

Pray Joyfully, 4:4-9

These admonitions to live joyfully, grow joyfully, and reconcile joyfully are noble goals. However, the Philippian congregation (and us) may wonder, "How?" Paul must have known that his words would lead to that question.

Therefore, he gives his answer: pray joyfully. Paul has woven the thought of joy all through this letter. Joy is the emotion that guides him through adversity and will guide the Philippians through theirs as well.

Paul's joy does not come from a naïve sense of optimism. Paul has dealt with his own struggles as well as the struggles of the congregation. He has spoken to the fear and anxieties of the false teachers. He has directly addressed the discord between two leaders in the church. He has spoken about the problems that threaten the fellowship of the congregation. Yet he urges them to rejoice.

The joy of the Christian life should be evident to believers and nonbelievers, to Christians and non-Christians. We should live in such a way that all who see us would want the same joy in them that they see in us.

Paul and many first-century Christians thought the return of Christ was imminent. In light of this immediacy, Paul calls for joy to be the order of the faith. We are to anticipate the coming of Jesus with forbearance, being alert and living with graciousness.

This joy is neither anxious nor fearful. It is not nervous or doubtful. It is not negative. It refuses broken relationships. It engages those who have bad behavior. This joy undergirds our lives and allows us to right wrongs, to heal hurts, and to worship fully the living Christ.

Paul's answer for how to live in this kind of joy is prayer! Prayer keeps us focused on Christ and straining for the prize. It keeps us positive and engaged. It is requesting God's joy to be our own joy. Prayer is the main activity that leads to joyful living. It is the one activity in which all the Philippians can participate. It is the one activity that will soothe anxiety and heal broken spirits.

Yet there is another activity that leads to joyful living: thinking on the good things of life. Paul is giving insight to the Philippians on how he has been living. He has focused on truth, justice, and excellence. As prayer and a positive mindset have benefited him, so will they benefit the church and its members.

We too ought to pray without ceasing, think on the goodness of God, and follow the example of Paul. As the congregation is faithful in these things, the blessings of life will be evident and their joy will abound. These virtues will bring us peace with one another. They will move us into the mind of Christ. They will bring us into the presence of God.

How do we address the messages of fear, anxiety, and worry in our world? We do so by praying without ceasing. We do so by claiming the blessings of life. We do so by bringing healing through reconciled relationships. We do so by claiming the joy of our salvation in Christ Jesus our Lord.

Life Questions

1. What choices do you make about life? Do you live in fear or in joy? Why? Who taught you to live as you do? What are the differences between living in fear and living in joy?

_____

_____

_____

_____

_____

_____

_____

2. From where does your identity as a Christian come? Who taught you how to follow Christ? What are the core beliefs of your faith? How do your understandings of living out your faith compare to the understandings of other believers?

_____

_____

_____

_____

_____

_____

_____

3. What happens when you disagree with other Christians? How do you express your differences in your congregation? How do you find common ground for living in community together?

_____

_____

_____

_____

_____

_____

_____

Joyful Living

4. What ceremonies do some people make into requirements for becoming a Christian? Do you agree or disagree with this? Why? What would Paul say about this? What do you say about it?

_____

_____

_____

_____

_____

_____

_____

5. How do you view "growth"? Why? What is scary about growing? What is exciting about growing? What keeps you from growing? What motivates you to grow? What growth needs to occur in your life right now?

_____

_____

_____

_____

_____

_____

_____

6. What is the role of memory in your faith development? What memories continue to motivate you to grow in Christ? What memories do you need to let go? How do your memories inspire you to strain toward the prize of Christ?

_____

_____

_____

_____

_____

_____

_____

7. What is Paul's view of conflict resolution? Whom sould be involved? Why? How? What would Paul say to your congregation? Are there people who need to be reconciled? Are there issues that need to be resolved in your church? Are there relationships that need to be healed? What are you willing to do to help bring resolution and healing?

_____
_____
_____
_____
_____
_____
_____

8. What are the joys of your life? What are the joys of your faith? How do these joys undergird you in daily living? Does your joy inspire others to be joyful? What do you need in your faith to grow more joyful?

_____
_____
_____
_____
_____
_____
_____

9. What fears and anxieties are rampant in our world? How does this climate of fear rob us of the joy of our salvation? What ceremonies in the church restore the joy of salvation? When is a time in church that you have been reminded to live joyfully? How can you continue to remember the joy of Christ?

_____
_____
_____
_____
_____
_____

Joyful Gratitude

Philippians 4:10-20

I mentioned earlier that writing personal notes is a lost art. In this age of text messages, e-mails, and social media message boards, folks seem to have forgotten how to write a personal message. I received a note last week from a friend who had spent the night with us. The note read, "Thank you for letting me spend the night." There was nothing else—nothing personal, no sentiment, no signature. At least the note was handwritten. I guess that counts for something.

My note cards are personal and personalized. The front of the cards read, "Wishing you a Rainbow and Watermelon Day!" Inside, the card is blank for me to write three or four lines of well wishes and thanksgiving to the recipient. I love to send these to friends. I like being able to say "thank you" in my own words and to be remembered for the personal card. The two symbols on the front of my cards are special to me.

The "Rainbow and Watermelon" line is a tribute to my grandmother, Nannie Prosser. Every Friday afternoon in the summertime, we had a watermelon "cuttin'" in the back yard of my grandmother's house. Attendance was expected, and unless you were deathly ill, you were present. These family times were special. I looked forward to them. First came the melon. Then my brothers and cousins and I would gather around Nannie for life lessons. She would tell us Bible stories and share with us the promises of God. One of the first promises I remember is the promise of the rainbow. Nannie taught us that the rainbow is a symbol of God's love for us. God has made provisions for us, and God loves us.

Nannie made us feel special during the time she spent with us. The rainbow and the watermelon symbols are my way of remembering her and honoring her. I wouldn't take anything for those summer afternoons in her back yard. I've wished often for just one more moment with her. I'm grateful for her investment in me.

In the same intimate way, Paul writes these verses as a personalized "thank you" note to the Philippians. He writes to perhaps his closest friends in ministry to thank them for the special gift. He writes to thank them for sharing Epaphroditus with him and to thank them for their prayers. And, as he writes, his heart overflows with joy for this special congregation.

Joyful Concern, 4:10

Paul walks a delicate line. This gift had arrived late. While not wanting to complain or chastise his beloved friends, he does make his point. Paul rejoices because they have "revived" their concern for him. For whatever reason, the Philippian congregation had missed an earlier opportunity to assist Paul's ministry. Paul delicately reminds them of this even as he rejoices in their help.

The Philippians were certainly partners in his ministry. They had been with him at every point, even in his suffering. They had supported him in his travels, his preaching, him imprisonment, and his impending death. Yet, while they were partners in ministry and beloved to him, they had missed some of the blessings of service. At some point, they finally make good on their offerings of support. Paul dances between praise and protest with a gentleness that reflects the intimacy of their relationship.

Yet surprisingly, Paul never uses the words, "thank you" (Craddock, 76). He is writing a deeply personal letter, and "thank you" seems shallow. How can one say such a simple word of gratitude for such a significant gift? He is overwhelmed and does his best to convey his heart of thanks.

Simply saying "Thanks!" didn't seem appropriate. The Philippians were deeper friends who deserved more than a one-line thank-you note! Paul rejoices greatly in the Lord for their help. While he does reprimand them gently, his joy is the overwhelming note. Yes, he is disappointed for a missed opportunity, but he rejoices in the goodness of God for their support.

These words of praise flow from his heart. There are no adequate words to express his response. Paul, much like the psalmist of Psalm 23, finds his "cup running over" and his emotions filled up.

What a blessing to care for others so deeply! What a blessing to be cared for by others so deeply! Both Paul the missionary and his beloved congregation were in a partnership of ministry, sharing the gospel of Jesus Christ. For Paul, there was no higher calling. For the Philippians, there was no better missionary.

Joyful Confidence, 4:11-13

Paul now turns to some of the most famous and beloved lines in the New Testament. He begins to explain to the Philippians his own strength. He writes to assure his friends of his appreciation and also of his independence (Stagg, 215).

Paul is a man of strength. He is a man of conviction. At one point, he was a learned Pharisee and a ferocious killer of early Christian believers. At one point, he was a blind refugee, exiled to Straight Street to contemplate his salvation. He claimed, some would say with arrogance, his salvation and elevation to apostleship. Because of these claims, he was greatly distrusted by the eyewitness Apostles and other disciples of Jesus. He has known the upside and the downside of life.

His humility is now more evident. He does not pursue their accolades. He does not seek to elevate himself to hero status. To the contrary, Paul emphasizes that he is a normal man who appreciates the goodness of life and has survived its challenges. In many ways, though elevated to hero status by the Philippians, Paul writes to make sure that everyone understands his humanity and his humility. He is in prison, after all. He has written consistently with both intimacy and distance, and these verses are no different.

Here he gives an overview of his own life in the context of his friendship. He's had experiences that have taught him how to live fully. Paul is proud of his independence and also grateful for the gift from the church. Paul has learned important lessons. He has learned how to be content in all of life.

This is a confession for which we should all strive. How different would our world be if we abandoned the consumer lifestyle? How different would our lives be if we lived out of contentment rather than want or desire? Paul owes his outlook on life to the strength he has found in Christ.

We should note that Paul does not deny the good things of life. He has been able to enjoy them. He appreciates the comforts that have come to him. However, he does not live only for the material things. Paul has experienced the rich side of life, but he will not be ruled by it. The finer things in life will not control him. He will not be held captive by selfish desires.

He is not asking for an offering from the congregation to continue living in luxury. He is in prison! He writes this thank-you note to say that he has been faithful, both to God and to their stewardship.

However, Paul does not seek poverty either. He seeks neither to be poor nor to be rich. His motivation is neither to make more money nor to live as a recluse. If one is too rich, the tendency is to become overconfident and proud. If one is too poor, the tendency is to become defeated and depressed. Paul desires balance in his life. He wants "just enough." He wants to recognize that Jesus is the giver of all good gifts.

Paul's motivation for living is to serve the risen Christ and to be found faithful in that service. Along the way, he has learned to enjoy life regardless of the circumstances. Paul is not a Stoic, one who finds contentment within himself. Nor is he an Ascetic, one who despises the material things of life. He also is not a Materialist, one who lives only for the finer things of life. He simply wants to be a balanced person, serving God faithfully to the best of his ability.

Paul wants his listeners to understand completely. The lessons of life through various circumstances have helped him learn contentment. However, this contentment is not found within himself, in his possession of earthly goods, or in the poverty of owning nothing. In all things, the only source of his strength has been Christ. He wants his beloved Philippians to understand this.

Paul is self-sufficient in all areas of life *only* because of the strength of Christ. Christ is the author and finisher of his strength. Christ is the strength that allows him to rise above hunger or plenty or wealth or poverty. We *can* do all things through Christ who gives us the strength not to be blinded by wealth, not to be defeated by poverty, and to be joyful in living life to the fullest.

He states emphatically that he is content in all phases and stages of life. I have never understood "contentment" (v. 11). I am rarely content! I'm not sure if my insecurities or my ego keep me from this. Perhaps my faith is just not deep enough. For whatever reason, this state of contentment has eluded me. How does one achieve it?

The joy that Paul has talked about before is certainly one aspect of living contentedly. Verse 13 is also one of the keys to this attitude of joy. Paul makes it sound simple, but for me, and perhaps for others, life is more complicated.

Many of us are burdened by our past and possessed by our possessions. Being content is as simple as living in the joy of Christ, but it is not easy. "Work out your own salvation with perspiration, aspiration, and celebration. Trust God and live on bravely. These are good words for such complicated days" (Prosser, 211). Contented Christian living comes only as we move into deeper, more intimate relationships with one another and with Christ.

Paul makes it clear that the joy that guides one to a full life cannot be achieved in isolation. While some in Philippi would argue, we cannot live only unto ourselves. No one is totally independent in living a life of faith. The joyful confidence of faithful living comes from the depth of relationship that the Philippians shared with Paul. But Paul emphasizes that the true joyful confidence of faithful living is rooted in Christ.

Paul is a pastor at the core of his being. He is teacher, missionary, and apostle, but, in these verses, he is pastoring his beloved congregation. He is fiercely independent yet craves relationships. He has an inner strength due to his own faith but also equally strengthened by the goodness of his friends.

Many of us think of ourselves as self-sufficient. We live in climate-controlled, electronically protected homes. We drive nice cars, wear nice clothes, and eat in nice restaurants. Life is "nice"! Sociologists reminds us that we seem perfectly comfortable in our "electronic caves," virtual communities, and remote-controlled relationships.

But Paul calls us to a more excellent way! As we live in the faith, hope, and love of Jesus Christ, perhaps we too can learn contentment. Perhaps we can proclaim with Paul, "We can do all things through Christ" (v. 13).

Joyful Sacrifice, 4:14-18

The generosity and sacrifice of the Philippian congregation goes back to the early days of Paul's ministry. Acts 16 and 17 give evidence of their material support for Paul. This young church would have had to sacrifice for these gifts. They had entered into a partnership with Paul "from the very beginning."

In fact, they were the only church that entered into a tangible relationship with Paul. Even when he was on mission planting the church at Thessalonica, the young church at Philippi offered monetary gifts and prayerful support.

Remember that this letter was repeatedly read aloud in worship. It was most likely a house church. There may have been no more than ten or twelve people gathered together. Their fellowship was

Joyful Gratitude

fragile, which is likely one reason Paul singled out Euodia and Syntyche earlier. Even in their fragility, though, they sacrificed joyfully to support the missionary who had started their congregation. Their sacrificial giving of money, prayers, and even a leader (Epaphroditus) was a source of joy for Paul.

Do you remember the pastor who baptized you? The church at Philippi had a special bond with Paul. He had helped form them into a congregation. As a church of young converts, they were zealous in living out their faith. They took seriously their witness, their service, and their stewardship. This congregation was the only one that bonded so closely to Paul. And as much as they loved Paul, Paul loved them more. Paul would remind them that through their gifts and the love of Christ, his ministry was able to abound.

And so, Paul says in v. 18, "Your account is paid in full. Your pledge has been met!"

The Philippians have given Paul much more than monetary support. They sent Epaphroditus to be a helper to him. They sent physical provisions to sustain him. They have been prayer warriors for him.

Notice that Paul uses the language of the business world in these verses. He is deeply spiritual but also able to speak the language of the marketplace. He uses imagery of records, receipts, interest, credit, profit, and accounts. He even says their account has been "paid in full" in his ledger. Paul is a pragmatic missionary, and he is pleased with their gift. Even more, he is pleased with the life lessons they have gained by giving.

Paul is proud of the Philippians, but he is also proud *for* them. The lessons they have learned in supporting him will serve them well as they continue ministry. Paul knows, as do we, that the blessing of giving is as special for the giver as for the receiver. Paul is grateful for receiving this gift; it allows him to continue giving. Paul is equally grateful for the giving spirit of this congregation, for it will carry them far.

He is not looking for another gift. He is not heaping words of flattery upon them so they will give more. Instead, he affirms that they have given him more than enough. To Paul, they are a "fragrance of sweetness, a sacrificial offering worthy unto God."

Surely these words echoed through the halls of the house church at Philippi. The people read, sung, prayed, and repeated them in gathering after gathering. In these verses, Paul affirms his beloved supporters in much the same way as he describes himself in earlier verses. Paul has strained toward the high calling of Christ. Through their loyal support, the Philippians have strained toward the same calling, following the model of their beloved missionary.

Joyful Blessings, 4:19-20

Paul now brings to a close his "hymn" of thanksgiving. He has poured out his thanks to this congregation in perhaps the greatest verses in Scripture, and still he has not said, "Thank you." That simple phrase is simply not enough for the overwhelming emotion that pours out of him. To thank them, he "sings" a doxology!

The only possible way to thank the Philippian church is to praise God. The only thing Paul knows to do is to give glory to God, *our* God and *our* Father. Surely, the greatness and goodness of God are best proclaimed in worship. Paul is singing praises to God for the Philippians' generosity, for his friendship with their community of faith, and for the saving grace given to them all.

Blessings abound both for Paul and the Philippians. Just as God has taken care of Paul, God will take care of the Philippian congregation. Paul speaks with "Christ confidence." He is not arrogant, but he is sure.

There is no way for Paul to return any of the support to Philippi. Paul is an imprisoned itinerant missionary who is in poor health and facing uncertain times. He is moved by their love and support of him, but he is living realistically too. Even though he probably will not return to visit with the Philippian congregation, he is proud of them. He loves them. He is grateful unto God for them. And so, regardless of what the future may hold for them all, joyful blessings abound.

Even from prison, even in his infirmity, Paul is joyfully confident that God is guiding. God will bless Paul even more than the Philippians have blessed Paul. God will bless the Philippians even more than Paul has blessed them. Their every need will be blessed in all the riches of God's glory.

But make no mistake. None of this will happen based on what Paul has done in his ministry. None of this will happen based on what the Philippians have done in their faithfulness. None of this will happen because of anything a person or congregation has done.

Instead, all of these blessings will come from God by Christ Jesus! Paul's admonition to us is in Philippians 4:8: "Think on these things!" His exclamation is that God will fully satisfy our every need according to the "riches in glory in Christ Jesus" (v. 19).

Life Lessons

1. When have you missed an opportunity to support someone? What were the circumstances? How did you know you'd missed the opportunity? How did you feel? What did you do to make up for the missed chance?

_____
_____
_____
_____
_____
_____
_____

2. How is Christ your strength? When have you relied upon the strength of Christ to help you through a rough time? What were the outcomes? What were the blessings? What did you learn?

_____
_____
_____
_____
_____
_____
_____

3. What are some blessings from God in your life that give you great joy? How do you give God the credit for these blessings? In what areas of your life are you in "want"? How do you give God the credit for your strength? What are your prayers for today?

_____
_____
_____
_____
_____
_____
_____

4. One of the issues most concerning the church today is consumerism. How are you a consumer? What does it mean to consume? How do you bring your consumerism to church? What are the dangers of being a consumer of religious good and services? What would Paul say to us about our consuming?

_____
_____
_____
_____
_____
_____
_____

5. Are you a consumer? Why? What drives you to live beyond your needs and be led by your wants? Are you content? How does one reach the contentedness of which Paul speaks?

_____
_____
_____
_____
_____
_____
_____

6. What is a "normal," balanced Christian? What does normal look like, feel like, taste like, and smell like? If you were to become normal, what changes would you need to make in your life? Which gives the better witness, the rich Christian, the poor Christian, or the normal (balanced) Christian? Why?

_____
_____
_____
_____
_____
_____
_____

7. How do you gain your confidence for joyful living? From whom do you gain this confidence? How are you inspiring joyful confidence in others?

_____

_____

_____

_____

_____

_____

_____

8. Do you remember the pastor who baptized you? What about this experience endeared the pastor to you and your family? Describe your baptism experience. Pray with thanksgiving for the pastor who baptized you and for the grace that flows over you.

_____

_____

_____

_____

_____

_____

_____

9. What do you need from God? How are you being a blessing to others? What joyful sacrifices have you made for the glory of God's kingdom? For whom are you praying? For what blessings are you praying?

_____

_____

_____

_____

_____

_____

_____

10. Upon what "things" are you thinking? What shifts need to take place in your thoughts? How can focusing on the riches of glory in Christ lead to deeper faith? How can this lead you to being more content?

_____

_____

_____

_____

_____

_____

_____

Joyful Benediction

Philippians 4:21-23

I don't like to say "good-bye." Something sad in that word keeps me from saying it. Good friends who have helped me grow in the grace of God are special. I don't like to think we may never see each other again. Perhaps we never will, but I don't like the finality of "good-bye." So my words for "good-bye" are "I'll see you when I see you!"

The day we boarded an airplane coming home from mission work in the Ukraine, we left a special family behind. They had cooked for us while we were there. They had driven us around the city. They had sacrificed time and energy to keep us safe and cared for. With tears, we hugged until the last moment to board. I never said good-bye to them. I just held them and whispered, "I'll see you when I see you!"

The day we departed from Cuba, we left pieces of our hearts there. Again, there were tears and hugs as we made our way to the airport. Again, we prayed together, hugged each other, and said no good-bye. "I'll see you when I see you!

You may think this is denial, but the pain of a final "So long! We'll never see each other again!" is too much for me to bear. The people who have touched my life are precious. Many of them live only in my memory now. Some of them have died. Some of them have moved theologically or geographically. But bearing the finality of the relationship is too much for me. My parting words remain, "I'll see you when I see you!"

Benedictions are a lot like my farewell. The final words of the worship service are spoken to encourage and inspire. These last words each week are shared to remind us of the presence of God in our lives. Benedictions remind us that the sermon is not the final word; that our good deeds are not the final actions. Benedictions remind us that death is not the final step of our journey. In a way, Jesus said this as he offered the Great Commission of Matthew 28: "I'll see you when I see you!"

That brings us to this striking benediction. Paul offers personal greetings and blessings to his beloved congregation. He has said all he needed to say. He has encouraged them, challenged them, and thanked them. Now he salutes them with a blessing in Christ.

A Joyful Congregation, 4:21

We might think that in a letter this personal, Paul would mention special people by name as he closes. The congregation is small and likely a house church. All the leaders have been significant in the church's founding, in the funding of Paul's ministry, and in the friendship they have continued to share. Paul surely would have known most of the names of the leaders. Yet he gives nothing personal in this verse.

Paul offers a general greeting to the whole congregation: "Everybody here says 'hey' to everybody there!" That's how we would say it in South Georgia. Paul resists the opportunity to mention names. We don't know who is with him. We don't know to whom he sends greetings. Paul simply greets the congregation and lets them know that everyone who is with him in his ministry sends greetings of love and thanksgiving to them.

Paul was probably like many who lead churches. We fear saying "thanks" to a group of folks because we might leave someone out. In thanking a few people, the last thing we want to do is offend someone by forgetting them in the list. Paul also knows that the congregation has changed some since his visits. There are probably leaders in the church now that Paul doesn't know. So Paul gives a broad, sweeping "thanks" to everybody. Better to be safe than sorry.

But don't let the fact that he doesn't "name names" lessen the significance of his care for this church. Paul's affection for them is real. By this time in the letter, the entire congregation knows they are special. There is no need for Paul to do a "roll call" of the membership to thank them. They already know they are special. They already know they are blessed to assist him. Following the preceding verses (Phil 4:10-20), the congregation knows the heart of Paul and how dear they are to him. They don't have to be listed individually; they've been listed corporately.

The nature of the congregation is its corporate identity. With a few exceptions, individuals have not stood out. The strength of this church is its fellowship. Paul knows this to be true. He greets them all in the intimacy of their fellowship. He offers a blessing in the intimacy of their faith in Christ.

Paul's affection for the church is grounded in Christ Jesus. Jesus is the foundation of their relationship. No matter what relationships might have grown between Paul and the Philippian congregation, Jesus is the common denominator. Paul never strays far from Jesus. He has made it clear that wealth will not define him, and poverty will not define him. Neither will Paul be defined by the relationships that are an important part of his identity. He will only be defined and can best be understood in the contentment and strength of Christ Jesus.

Paul stays close to the Christ throughout this letter. At almost every turn, he reorients himself and the congregation back to Jesus. He shares information and affirmation with the church. He shares challenges and appreciation. He calls for prayer. Yet for all the words he shares, he always returns to the foundation of their unity in Christ.

In keeping with his pattern, Paul ends the letter in the same way that he began: "To all the saints in Christ Jesus at Philippi." Paul loves the Philippian church. Paul loves Timothy and Epaphroditus. But Paul loves Christ Jesus more than he loves his own life. He continues to emphasize the centrality of this relationship.

A Joyful House, 4:22

As Paul is saying, "I'll see you when I see you!" he drops one last surprise. The saints that are in the household of Caesar also send their greetings. This is a grand revelation, both to the Philippians and to other believers who heard the letter. Paul doesn't use this greeting as a postscript to the letter. In the body of his benediction, he drops this tidbit of information that is a grand and exciting revelation.

The gospel of Jesus has spread into the domain, indeed the "house," of Caesar. What remarkable news! This must have been a tremendous affirmation about the vitality of the gospel for this struggling young congregation. Paul continually seeks to join together in unity the isolated outposts of Christianity. Paul hopes to build community among the congregations with whom he has worked. This information would have been a tremendous affirmation.

The "household of Caesar" was probably not the "home and family members" of the emperor. Though Paul may have had opportunity to witness to them while in Rome, and some would come to Christ in the years ahead, this phrase is not referring to family.

Most scholars agree that Paul speaks of those who served within Caesar's government. These are officials in the prison, the guards, and the civil servants with whom Paul would have had contact. Some of them were sympathetic to his plight. Throughout the empire, but especially in Rome, there were secretaries, low-level administrators, and slaves who were believers.

Scholars also agree that the "household of Caesar" would have been located throughout the region. In the provinces of the empire, these officials, military officers, and staff ministers would have been active in living their faith. Paul brings greetings from the believers in Caesar's Rome but also from all over his empire.

Philippi was one of these Roman provinces. In his travels, Paul likely met officials and soldiers who knew of his special relationship with the Philippian congregation. This is one other way of conveying support and affirmation from family members, friends, and colleagues who are serving all over the empire yet remembering this special church. What a powerful word of affirmation and blessing!

Christianity is evident in the heart of the Roman Empire. Three hundred years after this letter, Christianity became the official religion. Here, Paul gives early evidence of the presence of believers in Rome, in Philippi, and throughout Caesar's domain.

Joyful Blessing, 4:23

Paul now comes to the final word for his beloved friends. They have gifted him with monetary support. They have been gracious in sharing provisions to aid his journeys. They have even sent a church member to travel with him and share in the ministry. They have done more for him than any other church with whom he has worked. What does Paul have to offer them?

He gives them a simple prayer of blessing in the unity of Jesus. Paul knew this letter would be read aloud in worship gatherings. At times, the whole letter would be read aloud; at other times, only parts of the letter would be read. But it is fairly certain that the blessing would have been read aloud at each gathering. As each worship service drew to a close, the blessing of Paul would be shared.

As he writes, Paul imagines himself standing in front of the congregation. He visualizes the faces of the church members; he feels their embraces as they depart. So he gives them the simplicity of this blessing.

Paul knows that as they hear his words, they will be again renewed in the grace of Jesus. The greatest gift he can give them is unity within the grace of Jesus. What better gift than affirmation and unity in Jesus!

The letter ends as it began, in the centrality and strength of the Lord Jesus Christ. Paul says to his beloved congregation, "I'll see you when I see you! Until then, let your spirits be blessed by the grace of our Lord Jesus Christ."

What a joyful benediction! What a joyful gift!

"I'll see you when I see you!"

Life Questions

1. Who challenges you? Who was the first person, other than your parents, who challenged you? How did the person help you? What did he or she do for you? What five people have had the most influence on your life?

_____

_____

_____

_____

_____

_____

_____

2. Why do you think Paul didn't mention specific names in this benediction? Would the letter have had more or less universal appeal if he had been more specific? Why? What does this say to you?

_____

_____

_____

_____

_____

_____

Joyful Benediction

3. Which world leaders have had great impact in advancing the gospel of Christ? What can we learn from their leadership? How are you advancing the gospel?

_____

_____

_____

_____

_____

_____

_____

4. Who has a stronger witness for Christ—government leaders, celebrities, or everyday people? Why do you think this is so? What is your testimony? How has Christ changed your life?

_____

_____

_____

_____

_____

_____

_____

5. Have you ever gotten a personal letter from a loved one who mentioned greetings from other friends or family? How did this make you feel? What do you think the Philippians felt when they heard greetings from all over the Roman Empire?

_____

_____

_____

_____

_____

_____

_____

6. What is the best gift you've ever been given? What did this gift cost the giver? What does this say about how we value gifts?

_____
_____
_____
_____
_____
_____
_____

7. What gift did Paul give the Philippians? How much did this gift cost him? What does this imply to you about the best gifts we can give? Who is waiting on you to give them a gift similar to the gift Paul gave the Philippians?

_____
_____
_____
_____
_____
_____
_____

8. What is the best gift you've been given in this study of Philippians? What have you learned? What has changed you? What has affirmed you? How will you be different?

_____
_____
_____
_____
_____
_____
_____

9. Close in prayer for the goodness of your study of Philippians. Pray for your unity in congregational fellowship. Pray for your spirit of faithfulness. Pray for the gospel of Jesus Christ to continue making an impact in the world.

_____

_____

_____

_____

_____

_____

_____

Bibliography

Barclay, William. "The Letters to the Philippians, Colossians, and Thessalonians" (revised edition). *The Daily Study Bible Series.* Philadelphia: Westminister Press, 1975.

Bugg, C. B. *Preaching for the Missional Journey.* Atlanta: Cooperative Baptist Fellowship, 2010.

Craddock, Fred. "Philippians." *Interpretation: A Bible Commentary for Teaching and Preaching.* Atlanta: John Knox Press, 1985.

Dunnam, Maxie. *The Communicator's Commentary: Galatians, Ephesians, Philippians, Colossians, and Philemon.* Nashville: Word Publishing, 1982.

Foster, Richard. *Prayers, Finding the Heart's True Home.* San Francisco: Harper, 1992.

Lamott, Anne. *Traveling Mercies: Some Thoughts on Faith.* New York: Pantheon Books, 1999.

Lincoln, Andrew. *2 Corinthians, Galatians, Ephesians, Philippians, Colossians, 1 & 2 Thessalonians, 1 & 2 Timothy; Titus, Philemon.* Volume 11 of The New Interpreter's Bible. Nashville: Abingdon Press, 2000.

Moon, Gary. *Apprenticeship with Jesus: Learning to Live like the Master.* Grand Rapids MI: Baker Books, 2009.

Prosser, Bo. "An Example of the Traditional Bible Study Model based on Philippians 4:1-13." *Review and Expositor* 107/2 (Spring 2010).

Scott, E., and R. Wicks. *The Epistle to the Philippians.* Volume 11 of The Interpreter's Bible. Nashville: Abingdon Press, 1978.

Stagg, Frank. *Philippians.* Volume 11 of the Broadman Bible Commentary. Nashville: Broadman Press, 1971.

Still, Todd D. *Philippians & Philemon.* Volume 27b of the Smyth & Helwys Bible Commentary. Macon: Smyth & Helwys, 2011.

Wright, N. T. *Paul for Everyone: The Prison Letters: Ephesians, Philippians, Colossians, Philemon.* Westminster John Knox Press, 2004.

Pie

L' Abli → Switzerland
           Some in US